HELEN M. STEVENS'
EMBROIDERED GARDENS

David and Charles

FIG 1 ▲

'If you set it, the cats will eat it; if you sow it, the cats won't know it.' (Country lore) Cultivated since the mid 13th century, catmint, 'kattesminte', has had a place in the cunning-woman's garden for generations.

(title page) PLATE 1

Even if you are an indoor gardener, plants can be an inspiration. What is more evocative of the festive season that the poinsettia (Euphorbia pulcherrima) *suggesting a simple, but striking, design for embroidery?*
11.5 x 9cm (4½ x 3½in)

(contents page) PLATE 2

According to Chinese legend, from the tiger lily was born the first silk moth – the full story is on page 60, Chapter Four, The Garden at Night.
20.5 x 11.5cm (8 x 4½in)

A DAVID & CHARLES BOOK
Copyright © David & Charles Limited 2006

David & Charles is an F+W Publications Inc. company
4700 East Galbraith Road
Cincinnati, OH 45236

First published in the UK in 2006

Text and designs copyright © Helen M. Stevens

A catalogue record for this book is available from the British Library.

ISBN-13: 978-0-7153-2180-5
ISBN-10: 0-7153-2180-3

Printed in China by SNP Leefung
for David & Charles
Brunel House   Newton Abbot   Devon

Executive Editor Cheryl Brown
Editor Jennifer Proverbs
Head of Design Prudence Rogers
Designer Charly Bailey
Project Editor Lin Clements
Photographer Nigel Salmon
Production Controller Ros Napper

Visit our website at www.davidandcharles.co.uk

David & Charles books are available from all good bookshops; alternatively you can contact our Orderline on 0870 9908222 or write to us at FREEPOST EX2 110, D&C Direct, Newton Abbot, TQ12 4ZZ (no stamp required UK only); US customers call 800-289-0963 and Canadian customers call 800-840-5220.

CONTENTS

INTRODUCTION

It is impossible to say with any certainty when the first real garden came into being – some rough plot of ground around a primitive dwelling where non-essential, though probably useful, herbs shared the turned soil with, possibly, some purely decorative plants. Similarly, we can never be sure when the first true embroidery evolved: when stitches became something more than functional and stitchers took the first faltering steps towards artistic ornamentation. Perhaps the two events took place at around the same seminal point in human development. Certainly, in many ways, gardens and embroidery have progressed hand in hand ever since.

As discussed in *Helen M. Stevens' Embroidered Flowers* (D&C, 2000), floral and foliate designs are amongst the earliest motifs to have been chosen as embroidery designs. It is tempting to assume that women – who certainly carried out the majority of the stitching in early civilizations – would also have been the prototype gardeners. Whilst men were hunting, or undertaking the heavier duties associated with farming and cultivation on a grander scale, 'wise women' may well have taken the first steps to transplant herbs from the wild into plots closer to home. Who would want to roam the hedgerows for a clove of garlic or a sprig of pennyroyal when they could pop to a patch of land adjacent to their own door? With herbs important as culinary, medicinal and magical ingredients, and stitching an integral element in clothing, home-making and – as with plants – in 'cunning' or magical works, it is perhaps inevitable that the two became inseparably bound together. In later centuries medieval and Tudor knot gardens, the formal landscape gardens of stately homes, humbler gardens captured in homely Victorian samplers and the whole panoply of horticulture, from the naturalistic influence of Art Nouveau to the ubiquitous crinoline lady in stem stitch and French knots (Fig 2), has maintained and strengthened the bond.

Gardens are many things to many people. They are flowers and foliage, trees and shrubs, pools and rockeries; places in which to relax or exercise, to watch wildlife or create a fantasy of statuary. But every real garden – and every embroidered garden – is more than just the sum of its parts. As every landscape architect knows, by bringing together detail and broad sweeps of impressionism, close-up interpretation and distant blending of colour and shape – a diversity of dimension and perspective – we can create some truly delightful effects. In this book I hope to explore the garden through embroidery in a new and challenging form.

◀ *PLATE 3*

One of the most enduring images of the formal rose garden comes from Alice's Adventures in Wonderland: *'. . .the fact is, you see, this here ought to have been a red rose tree, and we put a white one in by mistake; and if the Queen was to find it out, we should all have our heads cut off. . .'.*

Roses, royalty and history have been linked since before the English Wars of the Roses in the 15th century, but the heady perfume of the rose garden still imports an atmosphere of relaxation. Here, the close-up framing features of a modern hybrid tea (left) contrast with the simpler blooms of an old-fashioned shrub rose (right). These, combined with the more distant features of the pink bush and white standard rose, create the first of our 'through-scapes'.
Embroidery shown actual size

23.5 x 23cm (9¼ x 9in)

FIG 2 ▶

My own version of the crinoline lady, whilst based on a 1930s image, is much elaborated and romanticized. The princess waits in the garden – outside her fortress tower – for the arrival of Prince Charming!

PLATE 4 ▲

The garden can be interpreted as naturally or stylistically as you choose. This fantasy is inspired by the legend of the Hanging Gardens of Babylon. Here, the through-scape is formed by the framing feature of peacock flowers (Moraea villosa), affording a magnificent glimpse of the peacock himself. Without the encumbrances of a realistic setting, rules of perspective can be ignored.

19 x 26.75cm (7½ x 10½in)

CONCEPTS

Whether you live in a city apartment, town house or country cottage, the scope for some gardening is always within your reach. Difficult, true, in a high-rise flat, but window boxes, balconies, even window-sills, can bring the outdoors to your fingertips and inspiration to your needle. And which of us at Christmas has not enjoyed the vibrant growth of a poinsettia (plate 1, title page) – for to my mind even pot plants fall inside the picket fence of gardening! Traditionally, the winter is a time for gardeners to sit back and plan next summer's profusion of growth and colour. It is also the time for the enthusiastic embroiderer to undertake her most ambitious work – long evenings with a good spotlight! In summer the gardener is out in the fresh air, for there is always something to be done in the garden. The embroiderer, too, can be tempted outside, for the pure, unadulterated light of a summer sky lends to silk and cotton alike a freshness, which even the most sophisticated daylight-simulation bulb finds difficult to match.

In *Embroidered Gardens* we will, of course, look at individual plants, flowers and trees, and the insects, birds and animals that are attracted to them, but we will also move on to a broader canvas of design, bringing together landscape and framing features in a format that I have called the 'through-scape' (Plates 3 and 4). This will allow us to explore the intimate anatomy of close-up elements whilst expanding our techniques and abilities into impressionism, pointillism and thumbnail sketches – whole new concepts of stitching. Summer and winter alike, the vibrancy and diversity of the garden will be examined and interpreted.

WORKING THE MASTERCLASSES

The five Masterclass projects explore a series of different scenes – from a simple cottage garden to a splendid stately home landscaped garden. Most landscape embroidery is undertaken on a pale background, but in the water garden and the garden at night we will work on a black ground, diversifying into special effects created with metallic and mixed fibre threads. In gardens for wildlife, butterflies, birds and animals enter the equation. If this is your first Masterclass book, you will find that each project is fully explained from transfer to completion, the level of expertise required progressing in sequence from simple to more challenging. Materials (page 88) and Basic Techniques (page 90) will give you all the information you need to get started and, at the end of each project, present your work to its best advantage. The Stitch Variations section (page 92) explains the various stitching techniques required for each project.

Readers who are familiar with previous books in this series will notice some changes in the templates and colour charts for the Masterclasses in *Embroidered Gardens*. Whilst the basic techniques that are needed to work the projects are similar to those in earlier titles, the introduction of landscape work will require some variation in their application – we will learn to miniaturize and simplify – making the reproduction and interpretation of the charts slightly different. More freehand work will be included (and thus omitted from the templates) and distant features, worked in fine, miniature stitching necessitate the addition of enlarged details to the colour charts. All these elements will be fully explained as the chapters progress.

The other colour plates and line drawings throughout the book are designed to elaborate on the subject of each chapter and can be traced off (using the same techniques as for the Masterclass projects) and worked separately. More experienced readers may like to include elements from these studies in the Masterclasses themselves – or substitute them for given motifs. The choice, as ever, is yours and you are encouraged to make each embroidery as individual as you are able.

SOME PRACTICAL ADVICE

In the many live Masterclasses that I have given, and in my Masterclass Lessons online, one query has arisen more than any other, and most commonly from garden enthusiasts – how can I avoid the silk or cotton catching and snagging on my fingers? The answer lies with your

fingers, not the threads. Soft skin and smooth fingernails are an embroiderer's most valuable asset. If you are a keen gardener, simply remember to wear your gardening gloves! Similarly, housework can cause havoc to the unprotected hand. However, the more stitching you undertake the smoother and more thread-friendly your hands will become. Using natural fibres, particularly silk, has a reciprocal effect: the emollients in the thread will polish your fingertips to an exquisite softness.

There is no reason why gardening and embroidery should be mutually exclusive. My own cottage garden, nestling deep in the Suffolk countryside bears witness! To many embroiderers, the garden is a source of inspiration and wonder. Visitors to the bird table, seasonal and permanent residents such as frogs and bats, the symbiotic relationship between certain plants and insects and, above all, the creation of a private environment in which one can either simply stand and stare or sit and stitch is an ongoing joy. To recreate that relationship in embroidery is to deepen the love affair.

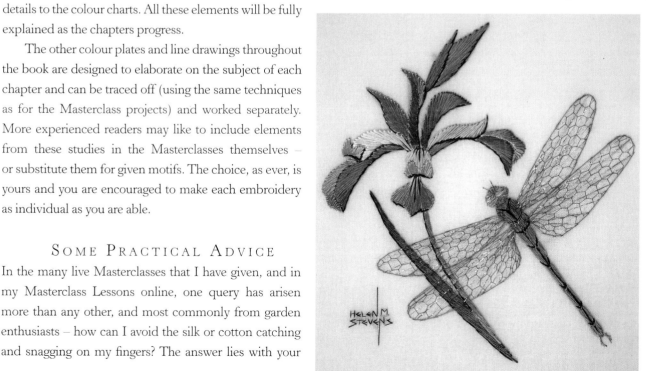

◀ *PLATE 5*

Many water features are best interpreted on a black background (see Chapter Two), but the magnificent emperor dragonfly (Anax imperator) *and the elegant iris work equally well on a cool, creamy base. The combination of ancient and modern fibres, silk and cellophane, make an interesting statement on any ground and capture the shimmer of a hot summer's day.*
9.5 x 10.25cm (3¾ x 4in)

HELEN M.
STEVENS

CHAPTER ONE

THE COTTAGE GARDEN

Like the rough, irregular count of an ancient evenweave fabric, a rickety trellis clings to a

red brick wall, threaded by a green silk of tendrils and stems. Foliage and flowers

intermingle in a patchwork of colour. Where will the garden path lead us?

Perhaps it is fanciful to believe that the cottage garden, as we now perceive it, is anything like the practical workaday plot of earlier centuries. Once, it was an essential part of country living – the fruit, vegetables and herbs were all important elements in the battle for survival, harvested in their season, bottled, stored and dried to eke out meagre winter rations. Yet many of those plants were attractive: fruit trees were laden with blossom in the spring, beans and peas bore pretty flowers and herbs were colourful and often sweetly perfumed. Even the most utilitarian garden must have had its delights – as long as the pigs or ducks did not escape their enclosures to run riot!

As time passed living became a little easier. Larger areas were put on one side for flowers. Herbs, once cultivated purely for their practical worth, were transplanted from inconspicuous spots into more visible locations. Areas once left muddy and bare for the driving of animals were grassed over and became lawns. The garden became a place where leisure time, still rare, could be enjoyed in peace and tranquillity. Today, the country garden has become the city dweller's epitome of rural living, a place of quiet repose where birdsong and the humming of bumblebees soothe the spirit. But gardeners know different.

The apparently artless tumbling masses of climbers, the closely packed flower borders and shady, secret corners all require careful planning and skilled execution. Indeed, a cottage garden is perhaps more like meticulously designed embroidery than any other

◀ *PLATE 6*

Country garden flowers have a natural tendency to mass together into interesting shapes and drifts of colour. Just as a distant bird can often be recognised by its 'jizz' – its stance and characteristic movement patterns rather than the detail of its plumage – so plants have profiles and outlines that can identify them at long range. Once you become familiar with the technique of extrapolating these 'identikit' features you can begin to create your own landscape elements (see Fig 3). Front to back: pink and white phlox, sunflowers (Helianthus), hollyhocks (Althaea) and lavender (Lavandula).

Embroidery shown actual size
24.5 x 21cm (9½ x 8½in)

FIG 3 ▲

Seed and plant catalogues are a wonderful source of design. Look at those massed plants offered as a 'bargain' – photographed in the distance they show their elementary outlines. Roughly sketched they typify plants of the various types: from the top, clockwise, sunflowers (large and open faced), umbellifors (such as chervil), irises (irregular), foxgloves (bell-shaped). Become familiar with these rough outline sketches before you try to translate them into embroidery.

FIG 4 ▶

Even in a rough close-up sketch, the individual blooms of the lupin are somewhat amorphous. In a highly miniaturized form (below) massed seed stitches (slanted upward) are idea for the flowers, straight stitches converging to central a point for the leaves.

type of garden. Plate 6 begins to capture its essence. It suggests that we leave the cottage through the framing features of honeysuckle and clematis – perhaps clustering around the doorway – and invites us down the warm sandstone path: the cat leads the way.

Once in the more distant landscape elements of the picture (see also Fig 3), we pass by tall, statuesque sunflowers, through phlox and hollyhocks to a bank of lavender where the path disappears and we are left wondering what lies beyond. As a child, I was fascinated by the idea of being able to walk into a picture and this is the effect that I have tried to capture in my through-scapes. This embroidery, however, like the garden it represents and the faded samplers of the Victorian world that it echoes, is carefully mapped out.

Honeysuckle and clematis are both long-time staples of the cottage garden. Climbing plants are generally popular as they hide unsightly elements, which, close to the house, may need to be camouflaged. Sweet peas are another favourite (see Plate 10). Climbers are also perfect as a framing feature for the embroidered garden – the interweaving stalks and stems create a fine framework to surround the landscape beyond. In Plate 6, I have chosen fairly complex shapes to emphasize the 'busy', crowded nature of the garden itself.

Radial and directional *opus plumarium*, stem stitch, floating embroidery, snake stitch, straight and seed stitching all feature (see Stitch Variations, page 92). The colours are cool and pastel – the deeper, more vibrant shades are reserved for the garden beyond.

Plate 7 uses a foreground feature to set the scene for the landscape. The ground-loving dunnock (*Prunella modularis*) suddenly notices that there is food to be had at the bird table. In the mid distance, to the left, poppies break the line of perspective; a thistle arcs around to lead the eye to the bird table, very impressionistic flowers, lupins (Fig 4) and daisies cluster at its base whilst a still-more-distant shrub cuts off the design to the right. The birds in flight add movement. Although there is no complete framing feature, elements 'contain' the subject matter within.

This containment is vital to landscape embroidery. In a photograph or painting the medium that conveys the image reaches and bleeds over the edge of the paper or canvas on which it is reproduced. Photographers and painters alike are often advised to find elements that frame their primary subject: an arching branch in the country, a road sign in

HELEN M.
STEVENS

◄ *PLATE 7*

In Chapter Three we will explore the wildlife garden but almost any plot has room for a bird table to encourage colourful visitors. The chaffinch (Fringilla coelebs) *in flight, right, needs little encouragement. The goldfinch* (Carduelis carduelis), *left, will more readily take seeds from growing plants, the thistle to the left offering autumn treats, while the dunnock will pick up fallen titbits. The distant pink and blue lupins* (Lupinus) *are one of the huge pea family (see Fig 4 and Plate 10). Here they are suggested by tiny, angled seed stitches.*

14.25 x 13cm (5½ x 5in)

FIG 5 ▲

Freehand work, whether unstructured, vertical or horizontal should hold no terrors. Simply and diagrammatically, as here, sketched grasses (left) are translated into straight stitches converging toward their base (right). The 'ground', sketched to the left, is conveyed by straight horizontal stitching to the right, whilst a climbing plant, corkscrewing around the tree, would initially be worked freehand in stem stitch, 'disappearing' behind its support as suggested by the dashed lines. The detailed portrayal of trees is dealt with in later chapters.

the city – something that will detract from a bland, 'mug-shot' feel to the finished image. But even if this not included, the work itself extends into the infinity suggested by the edge of the canvas. This is a luxury that we do not have in embroidery. Our images are finite and our designs must work on several levels: not only to convey the subject matter itself and to suggest an extended reality but also to encompass the whole.

In close-up studies we have no such problem: Plates 8 and 9 simply depict their chosen subjects. So, in a through-scape we can use similar bold elements to create our framing features, allowing the properties of outline and firm delineation to limit the spread of our distant subject matter, and in a smaller study, such as Plate 7, we must decide upon specific elements within the study itself to 'round off' the picture.

Once the design is created, then, like the gardener employing his well-learnt expertise in sowing, pricking out, growing on, transplanting and nurturing, the embroiderer must use her skills to capture the essence of the subject matter. In previous Masterclass titles we have explored many techniques that describe the realities of close-up work. Now we must adapt them to distant interpretation. In the Introduction (page 5) I mentioned the 'crinoline lady', a favourite design of the 1920s and 1930s, which showed a lady with bonnet (covering her face – no challenges there!) and parasol in a flower garden. In the United States a similarly popular design was the 'sunbonnet baby'. The motifs decorated a plethora of antimacassars, tea-cosies, tray cloths and cushion covers. The stitches used were those with which every amateur embroiderer felt comfortable: stem stitch, French knots, fly stitch and satin stitch. It was a charming, if unconvincing, tableau.

It was unconvincing because the stitches, not the subject matter, were the focus of attention. 'Isn't it clever', cooed a million stitchers, 'how a French knot can pass for a flower head.' Yes, it was – but the stitch should not have been the focal point. When we look at a watercolour, an oil painting or a statue, do we comment 'How brilliant – that pigment looks like a tree' or 'Wonderful how alabaster can imitate flesh'? No, we enjoy the overall effect. I believe that is how it should be with embroidery.

So, the techniques that we have used to such good effect in the framing features of Plate 6 and the studies in Plates 8 and 9 are adapted for use in the distant elements of Plates 6 and 7. The whole is fused in the use of stitches that capture light and shade, texture and form, focusing on the subject matter rather than the method.

There is one more golden rule that adds an impression of reality to landscape work: the contrast of horizontal and upright perspectives (Fig 5). Look at Plates 6 and 7 (and Plate 10, this chapter's Masterclass project). Elements that, to the eye, appear flat and in line with the ground, are worked on the horizontal; those that thrust upward, away from a baseline, are on a vertical alignment. This is a principle to which we will return again and again. To this disciplined stitching add the flexibility of freehand work – needed to overlay motifs that have already been stitched and would therefore overlay a transferred line – and we have all the techniques to create a study such as 'The Sundial', Masterclass One.

PLATE 8 ▶

*A surprisingly exotic plant that has become a
cottage garden favourite is the passion flower.
Passiflora caerulea is one of the most popular and
easiest to grow, given a warm, sunny wall. It will
need supporting – here a bamboo stick provides the
embroiderer with a contrast of texture. Flowers and
foliage are worked in floss silk, tendrils in couched
gold thread and the bamboo in stranded cotton.
The imagined light source is from the left – darker
shades of brown suggest shadowing toward the
right of the stick, emphasizing its roundness.*
9 x 17cm (3½ x 6¾in)

FIG 6 ▲

Less is more in impressionistic distance work. A centrally cored flower, such as the Convolvulus tricolour *(below) would be worked in mini-radial work in only five or six stitches, whilst the sweet pea, in a very small interpretation, would need only three or four – in effect becoming a tiny arc of graduating stem stitch (see Masterclass One).*

Sweet peas are the framing feature, close-up movement added by the holly blue butterfly (*Celastrina argiolus*) and white-tailed bumblebee (*Bombus lucorum*). Through the aperture we approach a tranquil scene: tall blue and mauve delphiniums, orange and white African daisies (*Dimorphotheca*) and pink geraniums – all cottage garden favourites – and, still standing proud after a century of following the sun's course, an old stone sundial, the same sweet peas clambering up its base. There are no techniques here that will overly challenge the embroiderer.

You might like to refer to Stitch Variations (page 93) to remind yourself of the principles of radial and directional *opus plumarium* – you will need both of these, plus snake and stem stitch for the close-up sweet peas. Now we need to miniaturize the techniques for the landscape elements. If you are working in fine floss silk, you will have the advantage of being able to work in a finer gauge for these miniature elements (see Materials, page 88). If you prefer stranded cotton or silk, continue to use a single strand, unless it is possible to split the thread into a strong half-strand (work a test piece first).

As you follow the step-by-step instructions for the Masterclass, work each technique as outlined in Stitch Variations. Where the prefix 'mini' is attached to a technique, reduce the thread gauge if possible and minimize the size of the stitch. Where, for instance, a sweep of around 30 or more stitches might be needed to describe the single arc of a sweet pea petal in close up, only three or four stitches would be needed in miniature (Fig 6), less if a broader gauge of thread is used.

The cottage garden is a unique combination of the practical and the purely decorative – a definition that could be applied to many aspects of embroidery. By drawing together the strands of detailed portraiture in close-up and impressionistic distance work we begin to unite the two in our own, special medium. Just as the passion flower (*Passiflora*) on its bamboo stick (Plate 8) unites the exotic and the mundane and the nasturtium (Plate 9) combines the attractive and the practical (both the pretty flower and the peppery leaf are a delightful addition to a crisp summer salad) we can complement one stitched discipline with another.

Practicality and decoration also apply to sundials in the garden, which have been used since antiquity to tell the time (Plate 10). Time for the first Masterclass: turn to page 18 to the template for Masterclass One and transfer the outline as given. Take a little time to familiarize yourself with the colour chart on page 19: remember that the shade names given are to enable you to choose your own colours depending upon your choice of threads – floss or stranded silk, cotton or other fibre. Then, following the step-by-step instructions and the detailed areas of the colour chart, work your way through the project. Don't be dismayed by the elements that you have to work freehand – remember these are no different to those that have a transferred outline but simply allow you a greater freedom of interpretation. Imagine yourself in that lovely, warm sunny garden. . .

PLATE 9 ▶

It is strange how perfumes have the ability to stir the memory. The sharp, spicy smell of nasturtiums immediately transports me to a garden in Cornwall, England, where my family took a house each summer during my childhood. Little did I imagine that I would one day be struggling to capture the strange, otherworldly shape of the flower in embroidery. Oddly alien blooms hover among leaves like miniature flying saucers. These are a real exercise in radial opus plumarium. Equally exercising to the gardener is how to keep them free from green and black fly!

10.25 x 21.5cm (4 x 8½in)

THE SUNDIAL

There is something magical about an old weather-beaten sundial, warm with the reflected sun in summer, icy to the touch in winter, faithfully reflecting the passage of the hours and seasons. Even in Looking-glass Land, Alice found a sundial, with plants and grasses gathering around its base and curious creatures making their homes in its shadow.

Work this sundial project on a pale background and allow plenty of extra fabric as the study needs to be mounted and framed generously. Carefully trace off the details on the template and transfer them on to the fabric – see Basic Techniques page 90.

TECHNIQUES

Where the prefix 'mini' is attached to any technique, reduce your thread gauge if possible:

• Stem stitch • Radial *opus plumarium*
• Directional *opus plumarium* • Opposite angle stitching
• Straight stitch • Snake stitch • Seed stitch
• Surface couching • Voiding

Work your way through the project, following the step-by-step details. Some small details do not appear on the template and will need to be worked freehand – these are no different to those with a transferred outline but allow a greater freedom of interpretation. The framing elements are worked in primary linear and filling techniques. These will be miniaturized for the distant elements. A range of textures may be useful: floss silks for the principal plants, stranded silk or cotton for the sundial and lawn. A touch of silver thread is used to bring the raised arm of the dial into prominence.

PLATE 10 ▶

Masterclass One: Embroidery shown actual size 23 x 22.25cm (9 x 8¾in)

Use a sharp pencil to trace the template to ensure all details are captured; when transferring, use a sharp instrument – pencil or stiletto. Some small details do not appear on the template and should be worked freehand.

See step instructions for enlarged colour charts of the background elements.

SUGGESTED COLOURS

	1	Black
	2	Soft green
	3	Bright green
	4	Blue green
	5	Blue
	6	White
	7	Ice blue
	8	Orange
	9	Yellow
	10	Peach
	11	Light peach
	12	Very light peach
	13	Dark grey
	14	Light grey
	15	Metallic silver
	16	Mauve
	17	Red brown
	18	Pink
	19	Green
	20	Yellow green
	21	Light yellow green

On the colour chart, tiny fields of colour that are obviously in the same shade as their neighbours are not always annotated individually. If necessary refer to Plate 10 to confirm these details. Work the freehand elements, allowing yourself some spontaneity. Again, the main illustration will guide you. Elements of distant subject matter are shown on a larger scale with the step-by-step instructions.

DESIGN NOTES

The imagined light source in this picture is from the top left and

this applies to both the framing features and the landscape elements –

refer to Plate 10 where necessary. Working butterflies is dealt with in detail in

Helen M. Stevens' Embroidered Butterflies, *D&C 2001.*

BEGIN WITH THE FRAMING FEATURES...

Shadow line in fine stem stitch in black (1). Do not
shadow the very fine tips of the sweet pea tendrils.

1 Work the stems, leaf veins and tendrils in stem
stitch in soft green (2). If you have a variety of
gauges, work the outer tips of the tendrils in a finer
gauge, gradually moving from fine to graduating
stem stitch as you work along their length.
Complete the leaves in directional *opus plumarium*
in soft green and bright green (3), applying the
opposite angle principle where necessary. Work the
broader stalks of the sweet pea in simple or reflexing
snake stitch, as appropriate, in soft green and blue
green (4). Work the butterfly's wings in three strata
of radial *opus plumarium* in blue (5), black and white
(6) respectively, and the body in ice blue (7) straight stitches running from head to tail.
Void between head, thorax and abdomen. Work straight stitches in fine black for the
antennae – one long and several short to form the club at the tip.

2 Work the sepals in lozenges of radial *opus plumarium* in soft green, blue green and bright green as indicated. Work the bumblebee's wings in straight stitches in fine black, angled toward the body. With the 'growing point' of the bee at its head (see *Helen M. Stevens Embroidered Animals*, D&C 2005) work successive strata of radial work in black, orange (8) and white to complete the body and block in the pollen sac in straight stitches in yellow (9). Refer to Plate 10 for legs and antennae – worked in black straight stitches – and add a tiny white seed stitch to suggest an eye.

3 Complete the flower heads in radial *opus plumarium* in peach (10), light peach (11) and very light peach (12) as appropriate. The 'shoe'-shaped petals will need acutely angled sweeps of stitching – the shorter the stitch slipped under its neighbour, the more acute the angle of advancement – see radial *opus plumarium* in Stitch Variations, page 93 and Fig 6, page 14. Remember to allow your stitches to abut the shadow line smoothly.

MOVING ON TO THE LANDSCAPE ELEMENTS...

4 Refer to detail chart (a) as necessary. Shadow line the sundial in fine stem stitch in black and block in the shaded areas in black and dark grey (13) in vertical and horizontal straight stitching as appropriate. Similarly, complete the rest of the structure in light grey (14). Don't void between colour fields except where vertical and horizontal stitches abut at the base of the dial – the shadow line suggests the break in planes. Surface couch fine lines in metallic silver (15) for the dial arm. In blue green fine stem stitch work the coiling stems of the distant sweet pea freehand, adding seed stitches either side of the stem stitch to suggest leaves in blue and bright green. Work tiny, shoe-shaped arcs of mini-snake stitch in peach to suggest flowers (see Fig 6).

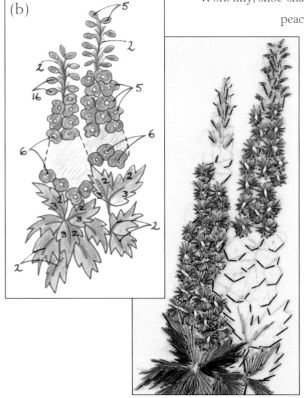

5 Refer to detail (b) as necessary. Impressionistic shadow lines are less detailed than their full-sized counterparts. Suggest the shadow line on the delphiniums with a few straight stitches in fine black on the underside of each flower and leaf, and more sparsely on buds. In mini-straight stitch in soft green work the bud stems, suggesting the buds in seed stitch in blue and mauve (16). Work down each spike completing individual flowers in mini-radial *opus plumarium*, allowing the outer edge of the stitches to overlap the suggested shadow line, giving the impression of a tiny shaded area behind each bloom. Work a single seed stitch in white at every flower centre. In mini-stem stitch work the leaf veins in soft green and leaves in mini-directional *opus plumarium* in soft green and bright green.

6 Refer to detail chart (c). Suggest shadow lines on the daisies in fine black straight stitches (petals and stalks) and mini-stem stitch below the centres (right). Horizontally, in mini-straight stitch, block in each flower centre in red brown (17) and work mini-straight stitches radially around each centre in orange or white, allowing the black shadow lines to remain visible between the stitches.

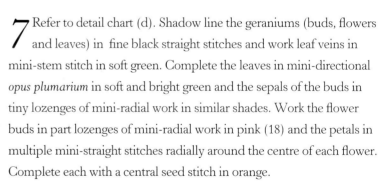

(c)

7 Refer to detail chart (d). Shadow line the geraniums (buds, flowers and leaves) in fine black straight stitches and work leaf veins in mini-stem stitch in soft green. Complete the leaves in mini-directional *opus plumarium* in soft and bright green and the sepals of the buds in tiny lozenges of mini-radial work in similar shades. Work the flower buds in part lozenges of mini-radial work in pink (18) and the petals in multiple mini-straight stitches radially around the centre of each flower. Complete each with a central seed stitch in orange.

Finally, refer to Plate 10 to work the lawn in horizontal straight stitching in green (19), yellow green (20) and light yellow green (21). Then, (in similar shades) in freehand vertical straight stitches angled slightly towards each other at the base to suggest clumps of grass, soften and infill between the plants, sundial and lawn.

(d)

CHAPTER TWO

WATER GARDENS

Amazing, how sound can suggest texture! The glamorous rustle announcing the arrival of taffeta silk; the cool swish of satin passing over chiffon . . . Glance up at the metallic whir of a dragonfly's wing and glimpse the cellophane brightness of refracted light, while the throaty rumble of a frog's croak suggests the earthy, green-brown dapple of camouflage fabric.

It has often been said that a water feature brings a garden to life. On the stillest day, when no breeze brings movement to foliage or flower, water is rarely still. The rising plop of a fish, the broken surface tension as a water boatman skates across the pond, even the strange jack-knifing motion of mosquito larvae mean that water is constantly alive with activity. It can be no coincidence that many watery motifs have become staples of the embroiderer's pattern book: from the Middle Ages to the present day, and from the Orient to the west, fish, water birds, aquatic plants and animals have provided inspiration both naturalistic and stylized. The format was never more popular than during the period of the Art Nouveau movement and Plate 11 pays homage to its principles.

The Arts and Crafts Movement, which evolved at the end of the 19th and beginning of the 20th centuries, was a reaction against the false, machine-lead fussiness of design that permeated the Victorian era. It promoted a return to natural, organic design sources and hand working, and penetrated every aspect of art and architecture, including garden design. Favourite structural and textile motifs included dragonflies and irises – whether lead by or following in their wake, the iris in its many forms became a garden deity.

In the wild, the stately yellow flag iris *(Iris pseudacorus)* likes its feet firmly in the water, or at the very least in wet ground along the edge of streams and rivers. Garden varieties,

◄ *PLATE 11*

One of the greatest joys of any water garden is its natural attraction for wildlife. Even a tiny pond repays its creation many-fold as insects, birds and animals are drawn to water and aquatic plants alike. A quiet moment with your sketch pad (see Fig 7) can lead to hours of interpretation. In this picture the foreground purple irises are echoed by their distant, miniaturized counterparts, the water lily and its pads similarly recreated. If possible, always use a finer thread in the same shade and texture to capture a more distant incarnation of a close-up feature.

Embroidery shown actual size
24.25 x 23cm (9½ x 9in)

however, of which there are around 300 species, are diverse: some insist on standing in water; some prefer dry ground. In plate 11, I have allowed the yellow flag to take precedence in the distance while using *Iris sibirica* as framing features. An arc of movement above is created by soaring emperor dragonflies *(Anax imperator)* while below, a water lily and frog – in his traditional fairy-tale pose on a lily pad – complete the stage setting. Here, then, is a 'natural' garden pond.

In Chapter One we explored the importance of framing features to encapsulate and round off the more distant scenery. Here, that distant element itself encompasses a central element bordered by softening, enclosing textural effects. The order of working the scenery is paramount. The water must appear to surround the plants whilst the grasses hug the edge of the pond. Worked in a fine floss silk, the flag irises and water lily flower and pads are initially stitched in detail, bearing in the mind the principles of miniaturization already discussed. Around them, in a softly twisted stranded silk, the water is built up using straight horizontal stitching – a darker shade of blue denotes the shadowed areas beside the bank and below plants. Long grasses are then suggested in slightly angled, straight-stitched stranded cotton at the base of the irises, and the fringe of grasses around the edge of the pond in similar cotton – worked over the water at the front and from the water's edge across virgin fabric to the rear of the pond.

In the foreground I have chosen to use the white water lily *(Nymphaea alba)* – like the flag iris a wild plant that has found its way into many gardens – and beside it, on the fleshy leaf, the common frog *(Rana temporaria)*. The same softly twisted silk used in the distant water is used here to suggest the close-up water effects; the lily and frog are both worked in floss silk. Simple radial work (with narrow arcs of stem stitch suggesting stamens) describes the lily petals. The frog, Mr Jeremy Fisher (a wonderful Beatrix Potter creation), is approached differently.

In *Helen M. Stevens' Embroidered Birds* and *Embroidered Animals* (D&C 2003 and 2005) we explored the stitching techniques used on diverse subjects, as widely sourced as

FIG 7 ▲

Subjects such as the frog have a very diffuse core, or growing point, around the blunt, stubby nose area – suggested by the dashed line. Once this is established, stitches should be worked towards it in the usual way (as indicated by the arrows), first Dalmatian dog spots (see page 94), and then the opus plumarium *flooded around them at appropriate converging angles.*

they were individual – from the old world to the new. It is perhaps an irony that in our own back gardens we are likely to encounter subjects that remain unexplored. The textural qualities of the frog belong with neither fur nor feather! As on a fish (see Plate 15, Masterclass Two, page 33), we need to convey a slipperiness that is, so far, alien to our effects.

Begin by establishing the flow the stitches (see Fig 7). Once this is decided, work the Dalmatian dog spots within the flow (see Stitch Variations, page 94). Work the eye in a roundel of radial work, centred with a large seed stitch in black, and a smaller highlight in white. Voiding around the eye and the body contours of the frog (where leg overlies belly and so on) flood *opus plumarium* around the spots, changing direction as necessary. Finally, fill the voids and complete the outline of the subject by surface couching metallic gold thread around the contours. Add tiny fans of silver metallic thread for the webs between the toes and fill the voided mouth with black silk. Here's as slippery a customer as ever plopped into the pond!

Textural threads can, of course, enhance these effects. In Plate 12 the great pond snail *(Lymnaea stagnalis)* is very simply worked in just two shades: a brown gold shell and gunmetal grey body. The former, however, in floss silk suggests the slightly reflective quality of the shell, while stranded cotton emphasizes a dull wartiness to the body. Both are then enlivened by a couching of gold and silver metallic thread.

Plate 12 plays with the effects of perspective to its ultimate. We are right there, getting a snail's-eye view of the

PLATE 12 ▲

The bog arum is related to 'lords and ladies', the wild arum lily, and sports similarly poisonous berries once the spectacular flower is over. Water features in any garden should be treated with respect – they can be a danger to toddlers even without poisonous plants! As a child, I was fascinated by the fat, lethargic water snails in our garden pond. Later, I was grateful to them for acting as immaculate models – a snail does not move so quickly that even the most laborious embroidery designer cannot catch up!

13 x 17.25cm (5 x 6¾in)

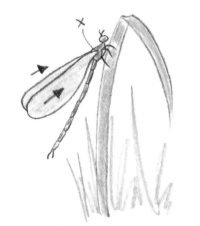

FIG 8 ▲

The dark bands on the wings of the banded demoiselle appear almost black in some lights by comparison to the pale blue fields on either side. Damsels hawk with their legs extended to catch unwary prey. The beautiful demoiselle (Calopteryx virgo) (below) has unbanded, purple wings. Broadly spaced radial stitches would converge, more simply, at the fulcrum point X, in the direction of the arrows.

distant waterscape, minute bull rushes and even smaller bog arum *(Calla palustris)* echoing the L-shaped arum flower and leaves in the foreground. Even without the contrasting elements of a landscape dimension, water plants provide a fascinating and challenging set of criteria – broad foliate sweeps of uniform colour complemented by delicately shaped and shaded floral bells and cups. The heart-shaped and arrow-shaped leaves of the hosta and sagittaria respectively, are good examples (Plates 13 and 14).

Whilst not truly water plants, hostas cannot tolerate conditions that are too dry, thriving best in the moist, shady spots often to be found in proximity to water. They are excellent ground cover and, as most gardeners find, often fill spaces where other plants are defeated by damp and darkness. More often grown for their showy leaves, I find the spiky pale lavender flower of *Hosta* 'Frances Williams' an attractive feature in its own right (Plate 13). Towering over the spreading foliage below, the bells open successively from the base upward, clustering attractively at the tip, quite as pretty as any campanula, and, if close to water, attracting a variety of insects.

Like dragonflies, damselflies are predators, hawking for prey in the shape of the tiny flying insects that thrive along the water's edge (Fig 8). The banded demoiselle *(Calopteryx splendens)* (Plate 13) is, to the emperor dragonfly, what a microlight is to a troop-carrying helicopter: lighter, more delicate, but not necessarily less deadly. Both are effective hawkers and the mayfly *(Ephemera danica)* (Plate 14) falls prey to them both.

In contrast to the broad, drooping, heart-shaped leaf of the hosta, the aptly named arrowhead *(Sagittaria sagittifolia)* thrusts upwards with all the energy of its namesake. Adaptable to various depths of water, its fast-growing leaves burst through the surface with all the velocity of missiles, spreading so rapidly via shoots that it can take over a small pond frighteningly quickly. For this reason it is often planted in containers so that it cannot get out of hand. The play of dense and light stitching in both Plates 13 and 14 epitomizes the dance of light and shadow across water. The solid sweep of *opus plumarium*

HELEN M.
STEVENS

◀ *PLATE 13*
A habit that identifies the damselfly is its
characteristic pose at rest, wings closed behind
its body (top left in this plate and bottom in Fig
8). Working to a fulcrum point at the base of
each wing, long straight stitches in pale green are
affected radially and interspersed with a band
of shorter stitches in blue to create the distinctive
strata of colour across its width.
14.5 x 21.5cm (5¾ x 8½in)

(radial on the hostas, directional on the arrowhead) completely obliterates the background fabric – the open-spaced, straight-stitched radial work on the wings (both on the damsel and mayflies) allows the background fabric to show through the stitching suggesting light, movement and translucence.

Dancing around the fountain in my own garden, in an ephemeral display of aerobatics, the mayflies reflected the

PLATE 14 ▶

In Britain during June and
July the handsome arrowhead
sports elegant white flowers,
each with a purple blotch
at its centre and a similarly
shaded pollen-bearing mass of
stamens. They flower best in
shallow water – conveniently
for the artist, as the delicate
blooms repay close inspection.
Seed-stitched anthers in a
slightly deeper purple than the
petal bases create an effective
cushion of colour.
13 x 21.5cm (5 x 8½in)

colours of the flowers around them, inspiring the polychrome interpretation in Plate 14. A friend's more formal garden pool was the catalyst for the study that becomes our second Masterclass (Plate 15). Again, the yellow flag irises are a focal point and grasses frame the backdrop of the pool, but here there is a more structured landscape architecture, and a more stylized framing element to the overall scene. An elegant veil-tailed goldfish *(Carassius auratus)* replaces the frog in Plate 11 with an added element of distant mystery – is the heron real, or a convincing garden ornament?

The needlewoven textural technique of laddering is the only foreground element that we have not yet encountered, whilst, in the distance, the flag irises incorporate a miniaturized version of shooting stitch to emphasise their markings (Fig 9): otherwise this Masterclass should offer no surprises. We will use needleweaving again in a later Masterclass (page 65). Here, it suggests the scaly effect on the fish. Work the veil-tail according to the step-by-step design notes: the body in perpendicular straight stitching, voiding around the various essential features (see Fig 10). Threading your needle with a similar gauge of the same shade of silk, weave across the underlying stitches, alternately picking up and leaving two or three stitches. Brickwork fashion, work down the body of the fish until the relevant section is patterned with the scaly, chequerboard effect. Any irregularities on the uppermost contour will be disguised by the couched outline thread.

As you become more confident in landscape interpretation, freehand 'needle sketching' will seem less daunting. In Masterclass One the contours of the ground features (different coloured grasses, shadows and so on) are delineated on the template. From Masterclass Two onwards, these are simply suggested on the colour chart. Use your own judgement and interpretation as to their extent. Similarly, the exact placing of angled grasses, the seed-stitched pyramids of the astilbe and the water coverage is left to your own working. You can, of course, refer to the main photograph in Plate 10, but why not use your own judgement? Change the angle of the perceived light source, for instance, allowing the shadows to fall in an alternative direction, suggest a breeze by toying with the direction of the upright grasses, or give the heron more chance of a successful snatch by removing some of the deceptively glistening straight-stitched metallic water effects. Make the picture your own with subtle byplays.

FIG 9 ▲

On this iris, shooting stitches, whether full sized or miniaturized, shoot out into the opus plumarium, *stitched away from the core – as suggested by the arrows. This gives a very subtle, but still noticeable, variation in the texture of the work.*

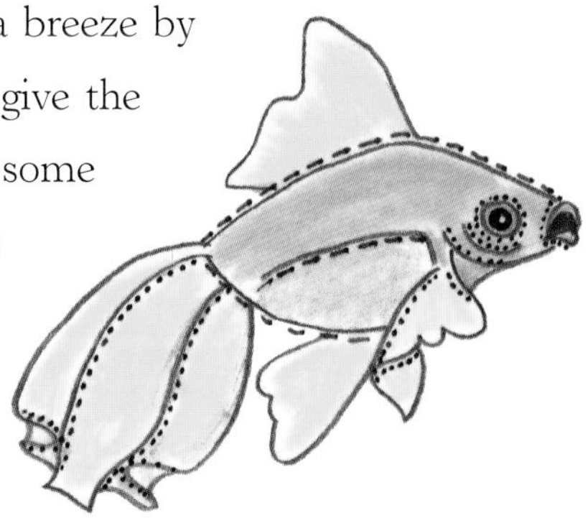

◀ *FIG 10*

When working on a black background no shadow line is used. To emphasize breaks in plane and contour, void between elements, as suggested by the dotted and dashed lines on the veil-tail, infilling those indicated by the dashed line with surface couched gold thread. The outline can be tidied in the same way. A fish on a pale background would need shadow lines on its undersides – these would replace the appropriate voiding and/or couching.

THE ORNAMENTAL POOL

Whether natural or tamed, water life adds a dimension of glamour to both the garden itself and its embroidered incarnation. Metallic threads seem a natural adjunct, adding splash and sparkle. Ethereal, seed-stitched pool-side plants such as the astilbe (far right) have their delicate underwater counterparts in the shape of fine stem-stitched water weeds, whilst a dripping strap-work leaf is echoed by the silvery bubbles rising from the goldfish's mouth.

Whilst it often seems more appropriate to work landscapes on a pale background, certain subjects cry out for a black setting – water is one of them. Below the surface of the water is an essentially alien world that can be captured most effectively on a dark fabric; you could try a deep blue as an alternative.

Divisible metallic threads are useful here: used entire they can be couched to outline the fish; separated into single, fine filaments they create its straight-stitched, radially worked fins and tail, as well as the dragonfly's wings. They can be finely couched to outline water droplets and bubbles, also suggesting the rippled surface of the pool where the fish dives to safety.

TECHNIQUES

If necessary, refer to Stitch Variations (page 92) to refresh your memory. Miniaturized techniques are designated, where appropriate, in the Design Notes:

- Snake stitch • Straight stitch • Stem stitch • Voiding
- Laddering • Surface couching • Radial *opus plumarium*
- Directional *opus plumarium* • Shooting stitch • Seed stitch

PLATE 15 ▶

Masterclass Two: Embroidery shown actual size 24 x 21.75cm (9½ x 8½in)

As discussed in the text (page 31) the extent of
horizontal ground and water features are omitted
from the template – and only suggested on the
colour chart, to allow spontaneity of stitching.

SUGGESTED COLOURS

1   Yellow green
2   Olive green
3   Very pale green
4   Sand
5   Dark sand
6   Black
7   Orange
8   Metallic gold
9   Pale blue
10 Metallic silver
11 Turquoise
12 White
13 Pale grey
14 Purple
15 Yellow
16 Bright green
17 Mauve
18 Blue green
19 Deep green
20 Pale pink
21 Deep pink
22 Dark grey
23 Dark blue

Refer to the enlarged details of the colour chart accompanying the Design Notes for precise shading of distant features. Where applications are obviously repeated in any motif not every field of colour is individually identified – use your own judgement! Refer to Plate 15 for an overall guide.

DESIGN NOTES

Whilst the imagined light source for the landscape elements of this design is

approximately top centre, the framing features allow a diffuse light source,

as though refracted and reflected by the water.

BEGIN WITH THE FRAMEWORK. . .

Work this (unless otherwise stated) in the full gauge of your chosen threads.

Reduce the thread gauge as you enter the landscape elements.

A variety of textures may be useful. Refer to Plate 15 for

suggested application of mat or floss threads.

1 Work the thick strap work of the large water weeds in simple and reflexing snake stitch in yellow green (1) and olive green (2) as appropriate. Overlaying the larger fields as indicated, work the fine water weeds in stem stitch and reflexing stem stitch in olive green and very pale green (3). In horizontal straight stitching complete the pond bed in sand (4) and dark sand (5), voiding between the contours of pebbles and so on.

2 Work small fields of massed black (6) straight stitch to suggest the inner eye and open mouth of the goldfish. In perpendicular straight stitching work the body in orange (7) and sand, voiding between the upper and lower body and to suggest gills (refer also to Fig 10, page 31). Outline the eye with a narrow roundel of metallic gold (8) and complete the mouth with fine snake-stitched arcs in sand. Needleweave laddering in orange across the upper body. Surface couch metallic gold thread around the outer contour of the body and in the voided body line. In fine metallic gold thread work radial stitching to suggest the tail and fins. Void to indicate the folded veils of the tail and between the lower fins. Infill two bubbles with pale blue (9) straight stitching and outline all three with surface couched fine silver metallic thread (10).

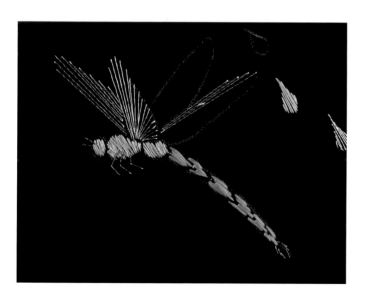

3 Work the wings of the dragonfly in fine metallic silver thread, in radial stitching, each towards its own core. In turquoise (11) infill the dragonfly's body in the stitch directions indicated (use a deeper shade of turquoise, if available, for the long, segmented areas of the body). Between each segment, and overlaying the upper body (see Plate 15) straight stitch chevrons in black. In fine metallic gold thread work a seed stitch between each segment, straight-stitched legs and antennae and tiny arcs of stem stitch for the tail 'claspers'. In fine metallic silver and pale blue respectively, infill the three water droplets, outlining the central drop in fine metallic silver in surface couching.

Moving On To The Landscape Elements. . .

4 Refer to chart detail (a) as necessary. Work the heron in mini-radial *opus plumarium.* Complete the first stratum in orange for the beak. Suggest the eye in black, and then work down the body in appropriate strata of white (12) and pale grey (13) incorporating the black markings where indicated and adding the head plume in an arc of fine mini-snake stitch in white. Work the legs in mini-snake stitch in sand and overlay straight stitches across the flow of the snake stitch in black to suggest leg texture. Work the small goldfish in orange and sand, with metallic gold fins and tail – stitch direction as indicated in Plate 15.

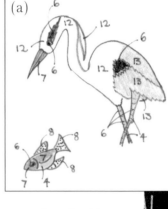

5 Refer to chart detail (b) as necessary. Work the inner strata of the flag iris flowers in mini-radial opus plumarium in purple (14) and flood subsequent strata of radial work around them in yellow (15). Apply the opposite angle principle where necessary. Add mini-shooting stitches in black from the purple into the yellow (see also Fig 9). Work the small upper petals in lozenges of sand, radially worked towards the core of the flower. Work the stems in mini-stem stitch in yellow green and the leaves in mini-snake stitch in yellow green and bright green (16).

6 Refer to chart detail (c). Work the stems of the hosta flowers and leaf veins in mini-stem stitch in very pale green. Add single or grouped seed stitches in mauve (17) to suggest the flowers and work the leaves in mini-directional *opus plumarium* in blue green (18) and deep green (19).

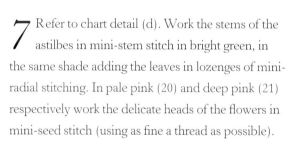

7 Refer to chart detail (d). Work the stems of the astilbes in mini-stem stitch in bright green, in the same shade adding the leaves in lozenges of mini-radial stitching. In pale pink (20) and deep pink (21) respectively work the delicate heads of the flowers in mini-seed stitch (using as fine a thread as possible).

Referring to the various details and Plate 15, work the stone border of the pool in massed horizontal straight stitching in dark grey (22). Use a mat thread to suggest the grainy effect of the stones and void between each stone. Suggest the lawn in horizontal straight stitching in yellow and olive green and the tall grasses in slightly angled upright straight stitching in yellow and bright green. In dark blue (23) suggest the water towards the edge of the pool and around the heron, flooding pale blue into the former shade as appropriate. Overlay the fish with fine straight stitching in metallic silver thread. Finally, highlight the eyes of the heron and fish with white seed stitches to bring our multi-dimensional water scene to life!

HELEN M.
STEVENS

CHAPTER THREE

A GARDEN FOR WILDLIFE

A sudden scuttling among the tawny, late-lying autumn leaves; thistledown glinting like scraps of gossamer silk in the sunlight; a tiny bead-like seed snapped up by an eager beak: a garden allowed to walk a little on the wild side is a joy. One man's weeds are another man's wildflowers. . .

Let's begin with Plate 16. I make no apology for the fact that, like many of the pictures in this book, it is based on a corner of my own garden! The landscape element of the design is small – it reflects the little niche between shrubbery and hedge that I allow to run wild: willowherb, nettles and burdock attract insects and birds, while long grasses mature into a tiny triangle of wildflower meadow where my cat stalks unwary prey. It is a microcosm of wilderness in an otherwise tamed country.

However restricted your gardening opportunities, there is room for a touch of the wild. Even a window box will throw up the odd interloper in the shape of a dandelion or a thistle. Allowed to mature, the tiniest seed or berry can provide sustenance for a bird or insect. If you are fortunate enough to have a garden incorporating old hedges and ditches you may well share your estate with a surprising variety of animals, which, unless you watch for the signs, you might never notice. In these days when, thankfully, we are encouraged to be aware of the environment, there are many good books available to help the would-be wildlife gardener. For those who split their passion between the garden and embroidery, the two can come together in an explosion of unexpected inspirational opportunities.

In previous *Masterclass* books we have explored the inter-relationship between plants, butterflies, birds and animals. What can be discussed in the abstract in books can come to

◀ *PLATE 16*

The greenfinch (Cardurlis chloris) is a sociable bird. Unafraid of human activity it favours garden trees such as yews and cypresses for nesting and repays the wildlife gardener for strategically left seeds by fine displays of enthusiastic feeding. Thistles, here the musk thistle (Carduus nutans) on the verge of seeding, and sunflowers (see Plate 6, page 8) are particularly popular. Lesser burdock (Arctium minus) (centre, middle), was much used by 19th-century landscape painters as its broad, shapely leaves made fore- and mid-ground perspectives interesting. Here, they disguise the scrappier foliage of the stinging nettle (Urtica dioica) and willowherb.

Embroidery shown actual size
24 x 22.5cm (9½ x 8¾in)

BRIGHT!

DULL!

ALMOST 360°
REFLEX!

FIG 11 ▲

A scribble straight from my sketchbook! What caught my eye initially was the swivelling action at the base of the thistle's leaf, but I hardly even bothered to draw it – just gave myself a reminder of what had made the impression. Then, just a very quick suggestion of colour density, and back to the business in hand – a walk with the dog!

life before your eyes in your own garden. Keep a sketch-book, notepad and a few coloured pencils on your kitchen window-sill: if, like me, your sink overlooks your bird table there may often be a scramble to remove rubber gloves before making a quick memo!

You don't need to be a great, instant sketch artist. A few quick lines, a daub of colour and a scribbled word can be enough to recall a scene later (Fig 11). There is no shame then in referring to good textbooks to get the details right, but your resulting design will be a true original: your own space, your own models and your own inspiration!

Willowherbs are one of the wildlife gardener's greatest assets. Growing with all the vigour and statuesque architectural merits of golden rod, they can be a joy throughout the summer and autumn. Be aware, though, they spread rapidly by both underground runners and seeds, so if you have neighbours who might not welcome their incursion, they must be kept under control! Both the rosebay willowherb (*Chamerion angustifolium*) (Plate 16) and the great willowherb (*Epilobium hirsutum*) (Plate 17) are members of the *Onagraceae* family, related to the evening primrose (Plate 17): in the late afternoon and at dusk they are all irresistible to hawkmoths. Hovering motionless, like dusty hummingbirds, elephant and bedstraw hawkmoths sip the nectar from all three – yellow, pink and green petals and wings mingling.

The petals of the evening primrose have a tissue-paper quality reminiscent of poppies. Almost translucent, this characteristic can be suggested by working in a very fine thread and allowing a little of the background fabric to show through the stitching. By contrast, the closed buds are more densely worked, as are the open flowers of the willowherb. The wings of the moths are worked in radial *opus plumarium*, on the same principle as butterflies' wings, stitches falling back to a diffuse core at the body of the insects. The bodies are broader and more textured than those of butterflies and laddering is used to suggest the chubby, segmented abdomens. We will work a hawkmoth in Masterclass Four.

Laddering is also used in Plate 18, 'From the Vicarage Garden'. Many a Victorian rectory was built a convenient stroll across the fields from the incumbent's medieval church, the meadow itself often church land let out for grazing. Sadly, true wildflower meadows are an increasingly rare survival in our intensively farmed countryside, but churchyards themselves have become havens for wildlife and occasionally the magic trinity of garden, meadow and churchyard can still be found in proximity. Where this happens nature has a broad canvas on which to play.

Fritillaria meleagris was still a relatively common flower of damp meadowland in the early 20th century, but draining, ploughing and herbicides have taken their toll. Now, however, it is a popular addition to the garden, occasionally in the border, but more often naturalized in grass – particularly if the soil is moist. It rejoices in a number of evocative names, snakes' head fritillary being

PLATE 17 ▶

Bedstraw hawkmoths (Hyles gallii) *(top) and elephant hawkmoths* (Deilephila elpenor) *are among the most attractive moths in Britain and welcome harbingers of long, late midsummer dusks. On initial inspection the wing patterns look complicated but by applying the usual principle of working each stratum in turn, beginning by those closest to the insect's body, it builds up simply and rapidly. A touch of gold and silver metallic thread for eyes and antennae adds lustre.* (See also Fig 18, Chapter Four, page 63)

11.5 x 17.25cm (4½ x 6¾in)

PLATE 18 ▶

*Yet another name
for the snake's head
fritillary is the Oaksey
Lily. As a child in
the 1920s my father
saw carpets of them
bejewelling the damp
meadows around the
Gloucestershire villages
of his youth: amethyst
and pearl studding lush
green pastures. Never
take one from the
wild, but if they are in
your garden bring one
to the drawing board
(see also Fig 12). The
chequerboard pattern
that we can recreate
in the technique of
laddering is actually
quite irregular – so
don't agonize over the
odd dropped stitch!
13.5 x 21cm (5¼ x 8¼in)*

the most obvious, but also the leopard lily and lepers' lily – the latter because of the supposed resemblance of its bells to the warning bell of the vagrant leper. It is a charming (though probably spurious) tradition that it was planted in churchyards by the 'lepers' window' to comfort the unfortunates as they waited for alms.

Plate 18 is an exercise in foreground and background texture worked in floss silk, twisted silk and stranded cotton. The lilies, worked initially in radial stitching to the core of each flower and then laddered to create the chequerboard effect (Fig 12) refract the light in floss. Grasses in upright and horizontal straight stitching, are worked in stranded cotton – mat to draw the eye back to the distant landscape, where a froth of young spring foliage suggests various tree species, again in floss. The church tower, sturdy and foursquare, is worked in a dense twisted silk, the texture imitating stone. As with the sundial in Plate 10 (page 17), the upward thrust of masonry is on a strong perpendicular.

It is tempting to think that once foliage becomes too distant to be entirely identifiable as individual species, its working is a uniform discipline. However, if we are convincingly to suggest its variety we must invest in a selection of colours and work in a diversity of angled and sized seed stitches. This technique and 'mid-ground' trees, showing boughs, branches and twigs will be discussed in later chapters. Around the church here, however, and possibly in the Vicarage garden (as it is in mine) one of the prettiest springtime trees is the hazel: golden, pink and green.

Spring comes early to the hazel coppice. In Britain, the common hazel *(Corylus avellana)* flowers as early as February, male flowers hanging down in clusters of soft yellow 'lambs' tail' catkins, female flowers like tiny green cushions with bright red stuffing bursting out in fluffy tufts (Plate 19). The common dormouse *(Muscardinus avellanarius)*, whose Latin name bears witness to his close association with the hazel, is provided, by its pollen, with a nutritious first meal after long hibernation. The wildlife gardener can encourage such visitors to take up permanent residence by allowing nuts and fruit to mature in situ – however tempting they may seem to us there are others with a greater need! Like the wood mouse *(Apodemus sylvaticus)* in Plate 16 the dormouse relies heavily on the autumn harvest to survive the winter.

Whether working on a dark or pale background voiding can be an important tool in describing composite features, such as the flakes of the catkins or the individual 'berry-lets' of blackberries (Fig 13). On the catkins, work each small feature uniformly, stitched conforming to a common convergence, each at its own core. On blackberries, and other garden staples such as mulberries or raspberries, work each berry-let at a slightly different angle to its neighbour. Light will catch the former in a continuous sweep suggesting a whole, sinuous lamb's tail, and reflect the latter as a series of separate entities massed together. Remember that your voids should be approximately the same width as the gauge of thread that you are using. Extra touches of reality can then be added: a peppering of tiny seed stitches to suggested disturbed pollen, or an occasional larger seed stitch nestling in the blackberries – the pithy core of the berry showing between the succulent purple berry-lets.

Whilst nettles and brambles might be anathema to the tidy-minded gardener, they

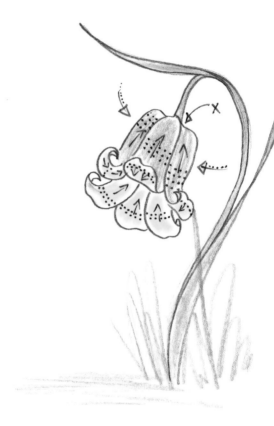

FIG 12 ▲

Continental Europe boasts a much wider variety of fritillaries than Britain. The Pyrenean fritillary (Fritillaria pyrenaica) *has a flared bell by contrast to the meleagris (Plate 18). The chequerboard effect, however, would be achieved in the same way – laddering, indicated by the dotted lines, worked across radial* opus plumarium, *the direction of which is suggested by the smaller arrows.*

PLATE 19 ▲

The symbiotic relationship of the dormouse and hazel benefits both. Many hazel flowers are actually pollinated via the whiskers of the dormouse, and when they bear fruit later in the year the protein-rich nuts are a favourite foodstuff. Whiskers, claws and general fuzziness is added to the dormouse as a last touch, overlaying other features to emphasize his furry texture.

11.5 x 9cm (4½ x 3½in)

are nevertheless peerless attractions for wildlife. Any eco-system needs a food chain; nettles and brambles are a sure and safe anchor. Over 40 species of insect are either completely or partially dependent on nettles for their food and shelter and of the nearly 400 members of the *Rubus* genus the true blackberry is just one of its invaluable fruiting varieties. While Plate 16 shows its autumn harvest, Plate 20 (Masterclass Three) features early summer blossom and buds.

Cross-pollination between species means that flower colour varies widely, from almost white to (as in Plate 20) pastel and deeper pink. They are nectar rich and can attract clouds of meadow brown and gatekeeper butterflies. Whilst not truly a nettle, the yellow archangel *(Lamiastrum galeobdolon)* is closely related to the red and white dead nettles and shares their reputations as guardians against evil spirits. In old cottage gardens it was planted by gates and can still be found running wild where country gardens border ancient woodland. Together with tall foxgloves, sedums and margaritas, the subjects in Plate 20 are irresistible lures to butterflies and bees.

In Masterclass Three the garden gate marks the end of the meandering grassy path (just a hint of green beyond the gate suggests that there is something out there), as it passes between differently shaped and structured herbaceous plants, the air alive with the flutter and buzz of insect life. The white wicket gate is simply worked in upright, straight stitching

– again the man-made element of the design adds a distinctive directional impetus to the embroidery, differentiating it from the natural. Light, shade and shadows are important to the depth of the piece.

As in Masterclass Two, you are allowed scope to change and adapt the scene if you wish. Before tracing off the template, consider omitting one or more of the butterflies and adding a bee or moth. You could change the colourway of the foxgloves – pink or white would give a cooler, more pastel effect. A small bird in flight (see Plate 7, page 11) would be slightly easier to work than the tiny insects if you do not have access to very fine threads and, again, the extent of the ground elements are left to your own judgement.

One final comment about the wildlife in my own garden: I often embroider outside and take my chances as to the dangers of bird droppings and the occasional pollen stain. Working a dusky blue cranesbill (Fig 14) in fine silk, it was an unimaginably magical moment when a real peacock butterfly landed on the almost completed flower and tried to find nectar! That I took as the ultimate compliment!

FIG 13 ▶

The hazel catkins (top) are worked as a series
of scales, each towards its own individual core.
They all converge in roughly the same direction, so
need careful delineation. On black, a small void
appears between each, but on a pale ground,
a fine shadow line would separate them.
The berry-lets of the blackberry, each worked
at differing angles, create their own voids
naturally as the stitches vary in direction. Being
dark purplish-black, a shadow line is unnecessary.
Tiny seed stitches in green break the colourway.

FIG 14 ▲

The dusky cranesbill (Geranium phaeum) *shares*
some of its colour with the peacock butterfly –
perhaps that is what attracted my welcome visitor!
Many popular garden varieties of geranium (great
ground-cover plants) are almost indistinguishable
from their wild relatives.

THE WICKET GATE

Foxgloves – the name comes from the Anglo-Saxon for fairy bells – have a magical quality all their own.

Whether in the wild, cultivated, or, as here, framing the portal between the two, they are stately gatekeepers.

Gatekeeper butterflies (Pyronia tithonus) *(left), and meadow browns* (Maniola jurtina)

(top and right), patrol favourite territories, defending them from interlopers with aggressive, dancing flights.

This picture is all about depth – we are drawn along the path, up to the garden gate and beyond; perspective becomes increasingly important. The tiny, darting bumblebees and butterflies around the foxgloves must be worked in a very fine thread – they are optional so, if you prefer, omit them altogether.

A variety of thread textures is, as ever, useful. The shimmering upper surface of butterflies' wings is, in nature, the product of light-reflecting scales, perfectly reproduced by the use of floss silk. Undersides

TECHNIQUES

Remember, where stitches overlay other techniques, such as straight-stitched grasses or seed stitches, do not work them too tightly.

A looser stitch will not distort the underlying threads:

- Stem stitch • Radial *opus plumarium*
- Directional *opus plumarium* • Straight stitch • Seed stitch
- Shooting stitch • Dalmatian dog technique
- Snake stitch • Voiding

are dull for the purposes of camouflage. Here, mat cotton is more appropriate to give the desired effect. Similarly, a dull sheen is affected for the paint of the garden gate with twisted silk. Become as familiar with texture choice as you are with colour.

PLATE 20 ▶

Masterclass Three: Embroidery shown actual size 23.5 x 23.5cm (9¼ x 9¼in)

HELEN M. STEVENS

Trace off the design with any omissions or alterations you choose.
Avoid using a ruler for the straight lines of the gate, as ruled lines
tend to transfer more darkly and are difficult to disguise.

SUGGESTED COLOURS

1. Black
2. Red brown
3. Very pale green
4. Blue green
5. Leaf green
6. Sand
7. Yellow
8. Pale pink
9. Deep pink
10. Orange
11. Rich brown
12. Dull brown
13. Brick orange
14. White
15. Bright green
16. Dark green
17. Pale blue green
18. Soft green
19. Purple
20. Mauve
21. Grey
22. Yellow green
23. Olive green

Freehand lines, though wavy, will disappear beneath your stitching. If you have a very distinctive 'wobble' simply incorporate it in your design – an old gate is probably less than immaculate anyway! Refer to the step instructions for enlarged colour charts of the background elements.

DESIGN NOTES

The imagined light source is varied: from the top right for the

framing features and top left for the landscape elements.

BEGIN WITH THE FRAMING FEATURES. . .

Shadow line the brambles and yellow archangel in black (1).

1 Work the stems of the brambles and veins of the leaves in stem stitch in red brown (2). Allow the stem stitch to thicken towards the base of the plant. Work the buds in very pale green (3) radial *opus plumarium* and the small leaflets in directional *opus plumarium* in very pale green and blue green (4) as indicated. Work the filaments of the pollen masses on the flowers in fine straight stitches in sand (6) and the pollen in seed-stitched black and yellow (7) (right). Complete each petal in a single stratum of radial *opus plumarium* in pale pink (8) (centre) and work shooting stitches through each in deep pink (9) (left).

2 Complete the larger leaves in directional *opus plumarium* in blue green and leaf green (5). Work thorns freehand at irregular intervals along each stem of bramble in short arcs of graduating stem stitch (around three stitches for each thorn should be sufficient) in red brown. Increase their size towards the base of the plant.

MOVING ON TO THE BUTTERFLIES . . .

3 Refer also to the pictures in steps 2 and 4. Work the wing spots in black in Dalmatian dog technique, subsequently flooding the appropriate colours around the spots. Beginning with the innermost strata, build up the wing patterns in orange (10), rich brown (11), dull brown (12) and brick orange (13) and work the bodies in straight-stitched rich brown for the gatekeeper and dull brown for the meadow browns. Work a seed stitch in white (14) at the centre of each black wing spot as appropriate (refer to Plate 20). Complete antennae and legs in black straight stitches.

RETURNING TO THE FLORAL FEATURES. . .

4 Work the leaf veins and stalk of the yellow archangel in bright green (15) in stem stitch and snake stitch respectively, broadening the snake stitch towards the base of the plant. Work the leaves in directional *opus plumarium* in leaf green, dark green (16), pale blue green (17) and soft green (18) as indicated, and the lozenge-shaped sepals at the base of the floral whorls in radially stitched bright green. In yellow snake stitch (radial *opus plumarium* on the forward-facing flower) complete the flowers and overlay as appropriate with shooting stitches or seed stitches in brick orange (refer to Plate 20).

MOVING ON TO THE LANDSCAPE. . .

Work a fine shadow line, as appropriate, in black on all features. Note: where two or more colours are indicated with an oblique (/) this indicates that shades are interchangeable.

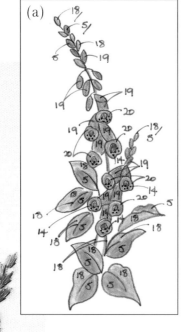

(a)

5 Refer to chart detail (a) as necessary. Work the stems and leaf veins of the foxgloves in mini-stem stitch in soft green, and the leaves in soft green and leaf green mini-directional *opus plumarium*, applying the opposite angle principle as appropriate. Complete the buds in lozenges of mini-radial *opus plumarium* in soft green, leaf green and purple (19). Work a tiny arc of mini-radial *opus plumarium* in grey (21) at the centre of each flower, surrounded by a roundel of radial work in mauve (20). Work the bell of each flower in mini radial stitches, each falling to its own core, in purple. Overlay the centre and lower lip of each flower with mini-seed stitches in white.

6 Refer to chart detail (b). Work the leaf veins of the sedum (left) in mini-stem stitch in olive green (23) and the leaves in mini-directional *opus plumarium* in olive green and yellow green (22). Work the flower heads in seed stitch in pale pink and deep pink and suggest stems in mini-straight stitch in yellow green and olive green. Work each margarita centre (right) in massed mini-straight stitch in yellow and surround each with a corolla of mini-straight stitches in white. Suggest the deeply serrated leaves with mini-stem stitch in yellow green and olive green.

(b)

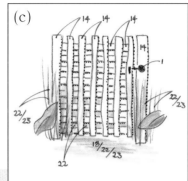

7 Refer to chart detail (c) and Plate 20 as necessary. Block in the latch in black straight stitches. Voiding around the middle ground leaves of the foxgloves, work the gate posts in long perpendicular straight stitches in white. In similar long stitches complete the uprights of the gate. In short perpendicular straight stitches complete the horizontals of the gate. Overlay angled upright straight stitches in olive green and yellow green to suggest grasses and work horizontal straight stitching in soft green, yellow green and olive green for the pathway before and behind the gate.

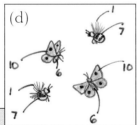

8 If you wish to work the distant bees and butterflies, refer to chart detail (d). Work the insects in miniaturized versions of the appropriate techniques in very fine thread according to the colour chart. Finally, infill the pathway, lawn and grasses with horizontal and angled upright stitching in soft green, yellow green and olive green as appropriate.

CHAPTER FOUR

THE GARDEN AT NIGHT

A black velvet sky spangled with chips of glistening shisha glass; dewy grass as cool

to the toes as fresh sheets; the still-warm perfume of night-scented stocks welcomes

you home, familiar as the lavender-rich aroma of the linen cupboard.

Your own garden at night is a place of intimate mysteries. . .

At night the garden takes on a new dimension. During the day visitors may have crowded laughing beneath the shady trees, in the evening a barbecue might have tempted guests with sizzling sausages but in the quiet of the midnight hour it becomes yours again. The cat steps silently into his own world, moonlight changes the colours of your favourite plants, trees cast unfamiliar shadows. In short, here is a whole new palette to tempt you, a new cast of characters to inspire, a new set of challenges.

As discussed in Chapter Two, landscapes sometimes need an 'excuse' to be worked successfully on a black background. Night-time, of course, is the perfect catalyst. Plate 21 glows with a luminous quality: touches of black and gold plied thread outline the honesty, fine metallic gold interacts with silk to capture the papery Chinese lanterns, grey and silver green stranded cottons suggest moonlit shadows. When entirely new criteria present themselves, experimentation is the key. Working this study I was confident that the landscape elements would translate readily from a familiar pale background – the stocks and tobacco plants are worked as they would be, with the omission of the shadow line – but the framing features were another matter.

Fore- and background elements of this study are linked by family. The Chinese lanterns *(Physalis franchetii)* (right), and tobacco plants are both members of the *Solanaceae* family,

◀ *PLATE 21*

Shadowfax, the white cat, is in his element hunting in the moonlight. In the silver-grey shade he merges with his background, fur reflecting the dim light. Embroidery stitches work the same way – as the light catches the stitches of his embroidered fur it reflects to give a three-dimensional effect – where voids have been left, and where there are irregularities in the stitching, a break of perspective is suggested. More subtle shadows are intimated by using grey and silver silk in areas that would, naturally, be in shadow. Pools of shade in the landscape element are suggested by areas of dark grey and silver green straight horizontal stitching – against a black background a 'negative' effect is achieved.

Embroidery shown actual size
23.5 x 22cm (9¼ x 8¾in)

*Honeycomb stitch (see also Fig 15) can be adapted
to mould itself into almost any field. By working
the 'radial' element of the stitch in the lower two
examples in the same direction as that already
established by the* opus plumarium *in the topmost
study, the flow of the design is established. Then
the cross stitches, 'sleepers', manipulate the radial
stitches into shape.*

5.5 x 7cm (2¼ x 2¾in)

sharing a rather dark reputation with their relatives such as bittersweet and deadly nightshade (see *Helen M. Stevens' Embroiderer's Year and The Myth and Magic of Embroidery*, D&C 2004 and 1999) whilst the honesty *(Lunaria annua)* (left) is related to the stocks *(Matthiola)*.

Chinese lanterns are usually grown only for the beauty of their curiously formed seed capsules, but I have always found the rather insignificant silver-mauve flower to be attractive (bottom right in Plate 21). The flower is succeeded by a round, brilliant orange berry that is completely enveloped by the calyx. The calyx swells to become the familiar decorative feature, its membranous, tissue-like skin gradually dissolving into a delicate network of skeletonized veining. As several of the fruit ripen successively on a single stem it is possible to see each stage of development – but how to capture it? I worked my first study on a pale background (Plate 22 and Fig 15).

First, the cage of the calyx was shadow lined in black, then infilled with narrow snake stitch. Then each segment of the lantern was completed in radial or directional *opus plumarium*, as necessitated by the shape of its field (top in Fig 15). Then, concentrating on the fibrous membrane of the lantern, honeycomb stitch was worked in place of the *opus plumarium*, and the immature berry was suggested by interspersed seed stitches (right). Lastly, another effect was tried – the mature berry was worked in radial stitching and then overlaid with honeycomb stitch. These techniques successfully tried, I felt confident to apply them to the main study, adapting them slightly to the black background.

Similarly, the honesty needed experimentation. Again, I felt that the flower (in this case, small, violet and scentless) deserved inclusion in the main picture, the seed capsules that succeed it requiring further study. Initially, as before, I explored them on a pale background (Plate 23). The flat, round seed pods are green as they begin to mature and quite opaque (middle). As they ripen the green outer valves can be rubbed off, revealing seeds adhering to either side of satiny inner septums. The mother-of-pearl, penny-like discs that remain can retain seeds that reflect dully through the translucent membrane. Working the outer hoop in shadow-lined fine stem stitch, I suggested the black seeds in massed straight stitches, working right over them in a single strand of fine white floss silk converging radially to a point at the base of the hoop. This seemed to capture their qualities effectively – on the pale ground. However, on a black background the techniques needed considerable adaptation. The fragile, woody hoop needed emphasis; the seeds disappeared completely!

In a single strand of very fine silver-coloured floss silk I recreated the radial sweep of stitching as in my experiment on the pale background. Around this was surface couched a

◄ *FIG 15*

The core of the Chinese lantern design is at the junction of the stalk and the lantern itself. Snake stitch is worked, sweeping upward towards that point (top). Radial opus plumarium *flows to the same point: this gives the key to the direction of the 'railway lines' (the first element of the honeycomb stitch, middle). 'Sleepers' are laid across the railway lines, brickwork fashion, pulling them apart and creating the honeycomb effect (bottom). (See also Plate 22 and for a fuller explanation of this technique refer to* Helen M. Stevens' Embroiderer's Year, *D&C, 2004.)*

PLATE 23 ▲

The honesty flower is a very simple affair – four
radially stitched petals with a delicate element of
shooting stitches at the centre (top left). This gives
way to the immature seed pod (centre), which
finally matures into the familiar glossy silver disc
(bottom). A keen flower-arranger's garden is
incomplete without this attractive plant. Sprayed
with silver or gold glitter it makes a superb
Christmas decoration – embroiderers can imitate
the effect by using fine metallic thread in place of
the white floss silk.

6.5 x 7cm (2½ x 2¾in)

line of black and gold plied silk and metallic thread. The resulting effect was simpler but more effective on the dark ground. Opposite angle stitching on the lower pods added to the three-dimensional effect.

Never be afraid to experiment – how else can we discover and expand new techniques? Plate 2 (page 3) is a design I created for a Masterclass project during a workshop. The template (recreated in Fig 16) was supplied blank and students encouraged to use their imagination and ingenuity to create differing textures and effects. Extensive use of the opposite angle principle on both radial and directional *opus plumarium* is necessary to give the realistic backward sweep of the reflexing petals, but superimposed effects and the choice of additional textural threads can present a number of unexpected variants (see Fig 17).

A fairy tale tells that one still night in China the tiger lily opened its petals and put forth its elegant pollen-bearing stamens. There was not a breath of wind, and the pollen became heavier and heavier until the blooms began to bow. Suddenly a breeze rippled through the flowers, the pollen stirred and began to fall, coalescing into a beautiful, broad-winged butterfly. But it was night-time and butterflies love the sun. As the lovely creature sought light it could find only silver beams of moonlight and the shimmering of the stars. Its eyes became bigger and bigger, its antennae softer and more feathery: the first silk moth came into being. Such was the inspiration for Plate 2 – for moonlight and stardust *are* magic! We explore both in Plate 24 and in Plate 25 (Masterclass Four).

Moths and mulberry trees share a heritage. Japanese folklore has its own version of how silk came into being. It tells of how once, a golden-haired princess was hated by her wicked stepmother and left to die in the hollowed trunk of a mulberry tree, set adrift in

the ocean. The princess, rescued by fishermen and released from her coffin, turned into a silk worm and wrapped herself in a cocoon of golden thread. After a while she emerged from the cocoon, not as a caterpillar but as a beautiful, pale gold moth. Flying here and there she laid eggs, all of which hatched into silk-producing caterpillars. The fishermen became rich and the fate of Japan as a nation was assured.

Silk is a natural fibre produced by many caterpillars (and spiders) and most luxuriantly by members of the silk moth family. The main silk used for millennia by humans is that of *Bombyx mori* – a species no longer found in the wild. It was domesticated over 5,000 years ago and is now unable to fly, walking only short distances on its preferred food plant, the white mulberry *(Morus alba)*. In the 1600s, King James I of England encouraged the planting of mulberry trees in an attempt to rear silkworms for home production of this valuable commodity. Unfortunately, black mulberries *(Morus nigra)* not white were imported: the silk moths were unimpressed and uncooperative, but many a stately home and university college has inherited beautiful trees, productive of delicious fruit in summer, stately and decorative in winter (Plate 24).

On a black background we can begin our exploration of trees in their simpler form, unclothed by foliage (though in

FIG 16 ▲

The size of the original of this design, Plate 2, page 3, is given in its caption on page 2. Enlarge this outline to the appropriate size, trace and transfer it in the usual way and experiment with textures (some are suggested in Fig 17). As well as possible laddering and surface couching, try the addition of seed or bugle beads on the stamens and anthers, or for the eyes of the moth. Colours, too, can be of your own choosing.

◀ *FIG 17*

Simple radial opus plumarium *creates a lovely effect on this lily, especially as the play of light via the opposite angle principle brings such a variety of shading effects (top): work your stitches in the directions indicated by the arrows. The effect in Plate 2 (page 3) is created by the addition of small seed stitches worked across the flow of the underlying work – studding (middle). Laddering could be worked on the underside of the petals to give solidity – work the needleweaving as indicated by the dotted lines (bottom).*

Plate 21 a young, summer-clad apple tree marks the boundary of the distant perspective): both winter and night offers an excuse for working on a dark canvas. To capture successfully the spirit of a tree we need to understand how it grows. I like to think of it as a network of streams, tributaries and rivers, all flowing towards a great estuary and, eventually, the sea: the tiny twigs and branches are the streams, larger boughs the rivers and the trunk the great estuary opening out to the sea at its base. Plate

Techniques for working the mulberry tree have been discussed in the text. The moon is stitched in closely worked fine seed stitches in pearlized blending filament, outlined with a surface-couched line of metallic silver thread. The same blending filament, stripped of its silky component and working in only the cellophane strand, is used to suggest the moonbeams, diffused through and over the branches. Angled upright and straight horizontal stitches suggest grasses and shadow.

12.25 x 12.25cm (4¾ x 4¾in)

24 illustrates the progression. We need to begin by working rough snake or broad stem stitch down the branches and boughs and feeding into the trunk, massing into a broad area of straight, relatively upright, stitching. From each of these large boughs, smaller branches emerge, again worked in an irregular stem stitch, feeding towards their bases – and from them small, fine, straight-stitched twigs complete the corolla. The progression is logical. We are introduced to the format in a slightly simpler form in Plate 25, Masteclass Four, The Magnolia Tree.

Masterclass Four is a somewhat stylized study (like Masterclass Two, page 33, also on black), leaning towards Art Nouveau for its inspiration. Magnolias have large, oval leaves and although they flower most prolifically in early spring – before the foliage emerges – sporadic blooms continue to occur on the fully leafed shrub throughout the summer, and sometimes a full autumn display offers a rare, Indian-summer treat. In Plate 25 we work branches and boughs as described above, replacing the 'twigs' with large centrally veined leaves. Among them nestle miniaturized versions of the magnolia flower and bud in the foreground. Other subjects that enhance our nightscape are a close-up of the tobacco plant (*Nicotiana*) (right), fuchsia (top left) and bedstraw hawkmoth (see also Fig 18 and Plate 17, Chapter Three, page 43). Tiny seed stitches in a metallic silver thread suggest a spangling of stars, and seed beads a scattering of early dewdrops.

Remember as we begin our study of trees (which we will continue through Chapter Five and its Masterclass) that their nature is essentially different to smaller, less structural subjects. Where, on a close-up study of a plant, stems and stalks need to appear smooth and sinuous – with your stem stitch adapted to such effect – on a tree we need an altogether more vigorous, sketchy, 'scratchy' character. For once, allow your stitches to be irregular, don't worry about 'jags' in your stem stitch, let vigour and strength be your watchwords.

I remember attending an awards ceremony in an ancient Cambridge University college. In the quad, mulberry and magnolia trees threw ghostly shadows against centuries-old brickwork, the air was heavy with perfume of night-scented flowers, and fuchsias 'Citation' (top left in Plate 25) and 'Party Frock' (below) danced in the breeze to the music of the celebrations. When you design your own embroideries, allow your imagination full rein – bring together your own recollections, folktales, myth, magic and memories. In the meantime, enjoy working The Magnolia Tree. . .

▼ *FIG 18*

Laddering is worked across the bodies of the hawk-moths to suggest the plump, segmented effect in the direction indicated by the arrows (see also Plate 17, Chapter Three, page 43). Both the bedstraw (top) and elephant (bottom) hawkmoths have impressive caterpillars, but it is the latter that gives it its name – the pinkish yellow caterpillar (right) looks very like an elephant's trunk, with the addition of two rather surreal eyes!

THE MAGNOLIA TREE

Movement and stillness combine in this study – the still, starry night sky filters through the tree's foliage whilst in the framing features the bedstraw hawkmoth hovers amid the bobbing heads of the fuchsias. Dewdrops gather in the angles of the close-up magnolia; the tobacco flowers open to pour forth their intoxicating perfume.

This is a full, lush design. Everything speaks of the ripeness of a summer night allied to its mystery: colours are rich and sensual, yet elusive; shapes are full blown but unconventional (could there be three more disparate flowers?); the tree is distant but the large, fleshy leaves are distinct and well defined. There are subtle touches of metallic thread. The main impact is achieved through strong, bold stitching. The magnolia tree is the only feature that is new to us. Work sequentially through the design notes, allowing each leaf vein, branch, bough and finally trunk to engage with its neighbour organically – let the stitches merge at the intersections of each element. The details of the colour chart suggest where colours flow together, but use them as a guide rather than a blueprint!

TECHNIQUES

On black, voiding is all important. The width of the void should be roughly equivalent to the gauge of the thread you are using, so it will vary on different elements of the design:

- Stem stitch • Directional *opus plumarium*

Radial *opus plumarium* • Shooting stitch • Snake stitch

Straight stitch • Seed stitch • Dalmatian dog technique

Surface couching • Laddering • Voiding

PLATE 25 ▶

Masterclass Four: Embroidery shown actual size 23 x 21.5cm (9 x 8½in)

Use a pale carbon paper to transfer the design on to your fabric. White and yellow carbons tend to be chalkier so be careful not to smudge designs as you transfer. Once mounted in your hoop, avoid touching the transferred design unnecessarily. Hold your needle delicately and do not rest your hand on the fabric as you pass the needle through.

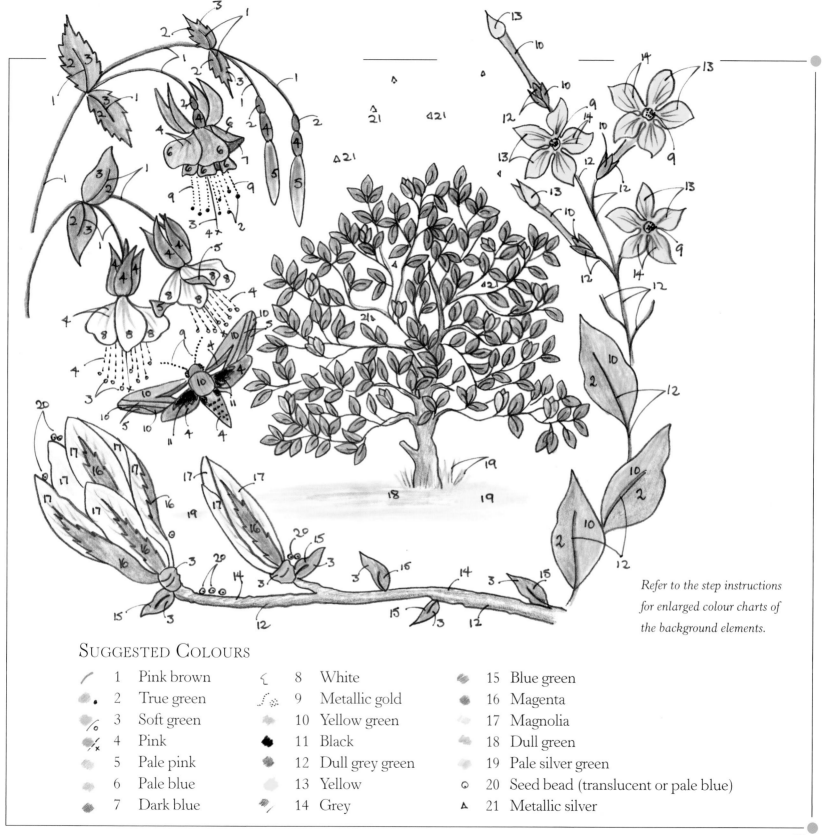

Refer to the step instructions for enlarged colour charts of the background elements.

SUGGESTED COLOURS

1	Pink brown	
2	True green	
3	Soft green	
4	Pink	
5	Pale pink	
6	Pale blue	
7	Dark blue	

8	White
9	Metallic gold
10	Yellow green
11	Black
12	Dull grey green
13	Yellow
14	Grey

15	Blue green
16	Magenta
17	Magnolia
18	Dull green
19	Pale silver green
20	Seed bead (translucent or pale blue)
21	Metallic silver

DESIGN NOTES

The imagined light source is diffuse – from above, but reflected across the design.

Pay particular attention to the angle of radial and directional stitching,

allowing it to catch the 'real' light effectively.

BEGIN WITH THE FRAMING FEATURES. . .

1 In fine stem stitch, in pink brown (1), work the stems and central leaf veins of the fuchsias. Work the leaves in directional *opus plumarium* in true green (2) and soft green (3) respectively. On the fuchsia buds, complete the calyx, upper and lower elements in true green, pink (4) and pale pink (5), working each segment in radial *opus plumarium* towards its own core. Add shooting stitches in pink to the lower bud petals. Work the upper elements of the topmost fuchsia flower ('Party Frock') similarly, adding the reflexing standard petals in snake-stitched pale pink. Work the lower petals in radial *opus plumarium* in pale blue (6) overlaying shooting stitches in pink. Complete the inner petals in dark blue (7).

2 Moving on to the lower fuchsia ('Citation'), work the fuchsia flowers in the same
techniques, in pink, white (8) and pale pink respectively, incorporating the opposite
angle principle where necessary. Add the stamens and anthers in
straight and seed-stitched metallic gold (9), pink, true green and
soft green as indicated (pay close attention to the colour chart!).
Turning to the bedstraw hawkmoth, work the inner strata of its
upper wings in radial *opus plumarium* in white and pink, flooding
subsequent strata around them in yellow green (10). Complete the
three outer strata in pale pink, yellow green and pale pink (again)
respectively. Work the lower wings in two strata of radial stitching,
in black (11) and pink. Work head, thorax and abdomen in broad
masses of straight stitching in yellow green and pink, incorporating
two Dalmatian dog spots in black to the upper, outer abdomen.
Add shooting stitches in pink to the thorax and laddering in black
to the abdomen. Work two large seed stitches in metallic gold for
the eyes and in similar thread surface couch the antennae.

3 Work the stems and veins of the tobacco plants in fine stem stitch in
dull grey green (12) and the leaves in directional *opus plumarium* in
true green and yellow green (refer to Plate 25). Work the long throats of
the buds and upper flower in yellow green – slightly angled radial stitching
falling to the radially worked lozenge-shaped sepals in yellow green and
dull grey green. Complete both the buds and flower petals in radial *opus
plumarium* in yellow (13), overlaying where appropriate with grey (14)
shooting stitches. Three large seed stitches in metallic gold at the centre
of each flower suggest the pollen masses.

4 Turning to the magnolia blossom, work the woody stem in massed straight stitching, in dull grey green and grey, allowing the strata and shades to merge towards the centre of the field (refer to Plate 25). Work the central veins of the small leaves in dull grey green stem stitch and the leaves in directional *opus plumarium* in soft green and blue green (15). Complete the basal cores of the flower and bud in lightly converging radial work in soft green, incorporating voids where indicated to suggest texture. Work elongated inner strata of radial *opus plumarium* in magenta (16) at the centre of the large petals, flooding outer strata of magnolia (17) into each. Complete the smaller petals, and part petals in magnolia. Add shooting stitches in magenta, radiating from the inner into the outer strata as indicated.

MOVING ON TO THE MAGNOLIA TREE. . .

5 Refer to chart details (a) and (b) as necessary. Work fine stem stitch in dull grey green for the central leaf veins and small branches. Complete the distant flowers in lozenges of mini-radial *opus plumarium* in magnolia and add mini-shooting stitches in magenta to the most prominent petals. Suggest the basal core of the flowers with seed stitches in soft green.

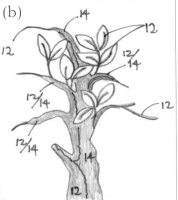

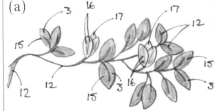

6 Continue the stem-stitched small branches allowing them to broaden and join the larger boughs. Feed grey stem and snake stitching into the whole – if you are working in a fine gauge, blend the shades together in the needle at the intersections and for the middle-sized branches. Sweep the stitching down and continue with upright straight stitching to complete the tree trunk, varying the shades to suggest light and shadow as appropriate.

7 In mini-directional *opus plumarium* work the leaves in soft green and blue green as appropriate. Allow the leaves to intermingle and overlap, separating them with fine voiding. Add horizontal straight stitching in dull green (18) and pale silver green (19) to suggest ground elements and slightly angled upright straight stitching in pale silver green for grasses at the base of the tree.

Finally, using a fine, self-coloured silk, attach seed beads (20) in appropriate places on the close-up magnolia blossom to suggest dewdrops, and add seed stitches in metallic silver (21) for the stars.

HELEN M.
STEVENS

CHAPTER FIVE

LANDSCAPE GARDENS

Green, brown and gold, the once tiny scraps that made up the patchwork quilt of England's countryside, neatly stitched together by meandering streams and byways, have long since become larger swathes of fabric. But in this modern collage there are still remnants of the old: irregular offcuts of ancient woodland, water meadows, manmade lakes, sculptured parkland and stately homes.

Embroidery is an art that demands patience. Like a successful garden, an embroidery takes time to evolve, to find its way from drawing board to completion. Most embroiderers, like most gardeners, have felt that surge of impatience when the right thread – or plant – cannot be found and experienced the times of drudgery when the 'boring bits' need our attention! Few, if any, embroiderers, however, have undertaken projects that they have no hope of seeing ripen to fruition, yet many of the great garden designers of past centuries have laid the ground-work of their creations, knowing that in their lifetime maturity will remain a distant dream.

As discussed earlier, the love of plants, gardening and stitchery has gone hand in hand for millennia. In the Pharaohs' tombs plantsmanship and textile art are depicted (almost) side by side, and to trace the liaison through aeons and civilizations would require more room that we have here! By the 10th century in England, St Dunstan (Archbishop of Canterbury) was using his herb garden as inspiration for embroidery design and by the time of the Tudors horticultural symbolism was commonplace in embroidered art. In 1570 Mary Queen of Scots famously sent an embroidered cushion to the Duke of Norfolk (whom she was plotting to marry) showing a garden vine and pruning hook with the legend *Virescit vulnere virtus* (Virtue flourisheth by wounding), suggesting that the barren vine (Elizabeth I) should be cut down and replaced by the fruitful stem – Mary herself.

◀ *PLATE 26*

The use of water, in the making of a modest or grand garden, is an equally effective device in embroidery design, but the art of capturing its reflective quality can be elusive. Its shape-shifting properties can best be suggested by changing the vertical to the horizontal: where the upward thrust of the temple is worked in twisted silk and the dome in floss, use the same threads but on the opposite alignment, interspersed with the straight-stitched water, to describe the reflection.
Embroidery shown actual size
24.25 x 22.25cm (9½ x 8¾in)

In the same year one of the first internationally famous gardeners was born – John Tradescant the Elder (he was succeeded by his son of the same name). He was also an explorer and importer of exotic plants, and by the time he was creating garden designs in the 17th century, Mary's son, James I of England had succeeded Elizabeth, bringing to fruition – in a way she might never have guessed – Mary's prophetic embroidery. A number of highly stitchable plants bear Tradescant's name (see Fig 19), woodcuts of his discoveries serving as potential embroidery designs for generations. Gardens continued to be principally formal, knot gardens survived from the Elizabethan era, walkways and avenues bisected geometric lawns sporting angular pools with fountains, trees in pots, statues and all the paraphernalia of elegant living. The tent stitched Stoke Edith Hangings (now on display at Montacute House in Somerset, England) captured the essence of the country house garden around 1720, as family and domestics disport themselves al fresco.

Into this world came Lancelot 'Capability' Brown, whose name has become a byword for the English landscaped garden, and the man who, above all others, changed the face of gardening on the grand scale. Born in 1715, Lancelot acquired his famous nickname by once commenting that he could see the 'capabilities' of an area for landscaping and it was, indeed, as well that he could 'foresee' them, for his schemes were as long term as they were extensive. Living into his late sixties (he died in 1783), he could have seen few of his masterpieces mature. The magnificent sweeping parkland of Blenheim Palace – surely his greatest work – was but dotted with immature spinneys at the time of his death.

Nevertheless, it is to him that we look for the typical landscaped garden – if there is such a thing – the inspiration behind Plates 26 and 30 (Masterclass Five, page 81). Broad swathes of grassland interspersed with copses of glorious native trees, including oak, ash and beech, naturalistic water features, channelled rivers and serpentine lakes served to create an idealized version of the untouched English countryside of which any

FIG 19 ▲

John Tradescant, 'that painful industrious searcher and lover of all nature's varieties', as a contemporary described him, gave his name to the generic of the spiderwort family – now favourite office plants. The garden can even come to work with you! The 'Wandering Jew' or zebra plant (Zebrina pendula) is shown here. Confusingly, these are not related to 'spider plants', those other staples of the top of the office filing cabinet!

nobleman might be proud. To this Arcadia was often added suitably elegant architecture: temples and rotundas, follies and 'ruins', again a tamed incarnation of the – this time ancient – wilderness.

Not only native plants were employed to bring the landscape to life, indeed, many of the shrubs and trees that we consider today to be typical of the genre are imported, among the most famous – or infamous – being the rhododendron. When introduced from Asia Minor in 1763 it was extensively planted for game cover. Spreading freely it proved difficult to control and crowded out many less sturdy shrubs and is now regarded as a weed in many areas – though the beauty of its flowers and glossy foliage cannot be denied. I have chosen it as the foreground and mid-ground feature in Plate 26, leading the eye to a distant landscape of lake, island, temple and woodland. The strong, waxy quality of both flower and foliage make a substantial framing feature – which need not encompass the whole of the study – echoed in the carefully structured working of the full shrub in the mid distance. In this chapter we will continue to explore the description of trees and shrubs in mid- and background locations.

Working on a black background (as we did in Masterclass Four, Plate 25, page 65) we have become familiar with the branching, meandering qualities of bough, branch and twig, each leading from its progenitor with increasingly fine stitches and threads. To this, on a pale background, we must now add the qualities of the essential shadow line, and finally, detailed foliage. Just as every close-up smaller plant has its characteristics, which we have learned to miniaturize by encapsulating its most obvious qualities, so trees and shrubs have their own persona. In the mid distance (as with the rhododendron) this is carefully detailed; further away it becomes more impressionistic and even more distantly simply a suggestion of shape and shade.

With a distinctive growth pattern such as the rhododendron this is fairly easy to establish. Having worked the framework of the bush (or any other tree to be portrayed,

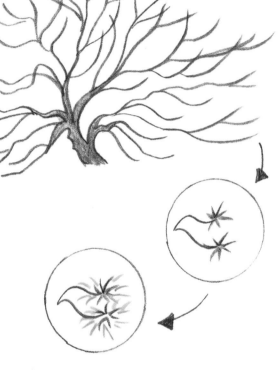

FIG 20 ▲

The rhododendron bush is worked in three main elements – trunk, large boughs and smaller branches (top). The flowers grow directly at the end of each branch: in miniature they are a whorl of purple seed stitches (middle). An outer corollary, or part corollary, of slightly longer seed stitches in light and dark green, suggests the supporting foliage (bottom).

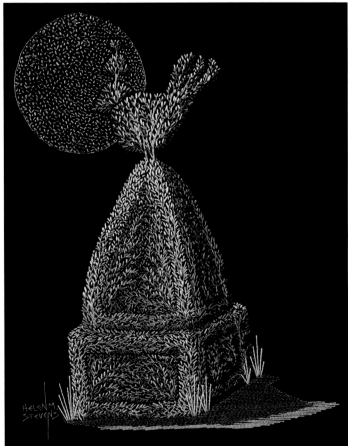

PLATE 27 ▲

It is perhaps perverse that the slowest growing
trees, such as box and yew, make the most
satisfactory subjects for topiary. As with
embroidery, the more you try to hurry the
project, the less satisfactory will be the result!
Small, densely growing leaves are obviously the
best candidates for ornamental clipping, but
they are difficult to suggest effectively even with
delicate seed stitching unless the framework is
carefully constructed first. The two disciplines
really are parallel.

11.5 x 14.75cm (4½ x 5¾in)

see Fig 20 (top) and Masterclass Five, detail 3) the character of the foliage must be established. Here, the large terminal clusters of blossom grow within the protection of radially positioned leaves – initially the bud is protected by a scaly sepal-like covering (see Plate 26, top left) – and this is simplified into sunbursts of seed-stitched petals, supported by a lower, outer corolla of slightly longer seed stitches suggesting leaves (Fig 20, bottom). Moving to the more distant trees on the island, these are suggested by massed, much smaller seed stitches, worked in random directions, tree and shrub types distinguished by colour and separated by areas of voiding. On the skyline to the left, even more distant trees become nebulous masses, straight stitched on the upright, emphasizing their almost architectural quality.

Between the mid-ground and background is the lake, island and temple, all worked entirely in straight stitching – horizontal for the water and land, perpendicular for the building. The eye is led still further towards infinity by a suggestion of the sky – straight stitched in two shades of pale blue.

The garden landscapes of the 18th and early 19th centuries were all to do with taming the wilderness, whether on the domestic or foreign front. Topiary had long been a craze, but now in more intimate garden settings, it became a national pastime. In the world of Jane Austin hardly a romance could have flourished without the private tête-à-tête in the ornamental walk. Box *(Buxus sempervirens)* and yew *(Taxus baccata)* are particularly well suited to this living sculpture. Visiting a formal garden, I was determined to try and capture the almost surreal quality of the clipped trees – Plate 27 is the result. Taking the principle of working the framework of the tree first to its zenith, I built up a fine filigree of branches and twigs to form a superstructure for the design. Each was then laboriously clothed with leaves in fine seed stitch, paying particular attention to the values of light and shade. The moon is suggested similarly to that in Plate 24 (page 62) – there is a dream-like quality to this embroidery.

Seed stitch, varied only by the length of individual stitches, can be used to capture the essence of a number of different textures. In Plate 28 I've used very fine seed stitching, colours finely graduated, to create the pockmarked skin of oranges. As the 19th century progressed, increasingly sophisticated methods of heating allowed hothouses to become features of many stately homes. Exotic plants (and sometimes butterflies) were imported and nurtured, allowing the Victorians at home to feel that they shared the experiences of those who, more adventurously, pushed the boundaries of empire. Fruit of many kinds had long been staples of the embroidery pattern book (Fig 21). As the Victorian era drew to a close, however, the well-established tenets of formal design began to slip and a freer style to emerge. The coming of the Arts and Crafts Movement was a wind of change that blew through gardens and embroidery alike.

◀ *FIG 21*

Four different tent stitch embroidery designs of the late 16th and early 17th century have been combined here to create a single stylized pattern in Jacobean style – cherry, pear, plum and blackcurrant. In later centuries more exotic fruits were added to the embroiderer's pattern book.

PLATE 28 ▲

The Seville orange (Citrus aurantium) *shares something of its history with silk, as it first came to Europe from the Far East around the year 1000 in the panniers of beasts using the Silk Route – some 500 years before the sweet orange was introduced from China. Usually too sour to eat raw, it makes excellent preserve and was a staple of the medieval lady's stillroom. The butterfly is an imaginative addition in the manner of Jacobean stump work design.*
10.25 x 16cm (4 x 6¼in)

In the early part of her life Gertrude Jekyll's greatest passions had been for embroidery and painting. As progressive myopia made these more difficult to achieve, she turned to gardening and it is perhaps ironic that this, her 'second choice', should be the art for which she is chiefly remembered. Born in 1843, she was a contemporary of William Morris, whose association with embroidery is well documented, and with his influence and in partnership with the architect Sir Edward Lutyens, her landscaped gardens were truly idealized tapestries of the English countryside. Jekyll's designs are best known for their glorious herbaceous borders with colour schemes running from cold (white

PLATE 29 ▶

A 'candle in the wind' – I love this design! It is so simple and yet so evocative of an English spring. Each of the flower heads, massed collectively to form the spike, is worked petal by petal in two strata of radial opus plumarium. *White filaments in fine floss silk are then worked over the underlying stitches, each tipped with a seed stitch in deep orange. You can almost feel the breeze scattering the pollen.*

14 x 14.75cm (5½ x 5¾in)

and icy pink) to hot (red and orange) and back to cold again. In Plate 29 I have tried to capture this feeling in a microcosm.

The candle-like flowers of the horse chestnut *(Aesculus hippocastanum)* are principally white but the central area of the corolla, beginning yellow, progresses through shades of orange, pink and crimson, and with all stages present at the same time the result is a tour de force. Offset by the lush, young, bright green leaves it is a Jekyll design in miniature. A white-tailed bumblebee, scenting the heady nectar, is attracted to the candle like a moth to a flame.

The addition of movement in the shape of an insect or animal does more than create incidental interest to a study. The Arts and Crafts Movement looked back to an idealized Middle Ages for its inspiration – a time when artisanship was a blend of many disciplines – art, craft, storytelling – none mutually exclusive. In our final Masterclass I have brought something of that ethos to our picture. The addition of the deer tells us a story.

Fallow deer *(Dama dama)* were introduced to medieval Britain by the Normans (though some may have been in captivity with the Romans) and lived virtually feral for centuries in ancient forests where they were hunted for sport and food. Later, becoming the first choice for gracing the parks of stately homes, they attained the status of 'pets' to the nobility, tamed along with their environment. Now, as we begin to understand more fully the interaction between the wild and domestic spheres of our landscape it is still a thrill to see them at dawn or dusk, grazing beside a wild spinney or resting in the deer-park (Fig 22). Either seems to be their 'natural' environment.

Perhaps our gardens, too, have come full circle. From a partly tamed scrap of land growing herbs conveniently adjacent to a cottage, to the huge rolling acres of stately landscaped grounds, gardens are a way of bringing nature to our doorstep. And with nature our finest model and inspiration, how can the embroiderer fail to be enthusiastic?

FIG 22 ▲

In the dappled shade of the hedgerow or copse, the markings of a fawn afford fine camouflage. Just as in the miniaturized version (Plate 30), head and body would be shadow lined, Dalmatian dog spots worked in the flow of the surrounding radial opus plumarium, and the whole motif softened by straight stitching across voids and outlines. Finally, the fawn is snuggled into straight-stitched grasses to complete his hiding place.

THE DEER-PARK

Yellow, gold and green, the early sunshine illuminates a fresh spring morning. Birds are in flight

and the fallow deer, startled by some sudden movement, scatter across the undulating parkland.

The flowers of the azalea (Azalea mollis *or* Rhododendron japonicum) *extend the sunlit theme into*

the framing feature, bright young foliage arching like candelabra to support their soft inflorescence.

Here, for the first time in a Masterclass, we extend the view to the horizon, elements becoming increasingly impressionistic as the view sweeps away. As ever, a variety of textures would be useful: twisted or stranded cotton or silk for the grassland – the same texture used on the most distant trees to create a density of effect. Similarly, a mat thread is best suited to architectural features – in this case the temple. The finest floss silk is needed for the suggestion of the sky.

TECHNIQUES

There are no stitches here that we have not already explored, but remember to vary their application. Seed stitches can be small and rounded or slightly longer as appropriate to the element to be described:

- Stem stitch • Snake stitch • Directional *opus plumarium*
- Radial *opus plumarium* • Seed stitch • Straight stitch Dalmatian dog technique • Voiding

The fallow deer are worked in miniaturized versions of radial *opus plumarium* with the incorporation of Dalmatian dog technique. You will find it useful to refer to *Helen M. Stevens' Embroidered Animals* (D&C, 2005) to recap animal portraiture principles. Tiny details are all important – even on this minute scale the addition of a highlight to the eye brings subjects to life.

PLATE 30 ▶

Masterclass Five: Embroidery shown actual size 23.5 x 18cm (9¼ x 7in)

HELEN M.
STEVENS

Certain elements of the groundwork have been delineated – i.e. the suggestion of the pathway across the lawns from the temple mount and the rutting rings around the base of the oak tree and to the forefront of the deer. These may be traced and transferred to give a basis for the more extensive ground features, which, as ever, should be allowed to grow freely as you work. A suggestion of their placement and shading is given on the colour chart.

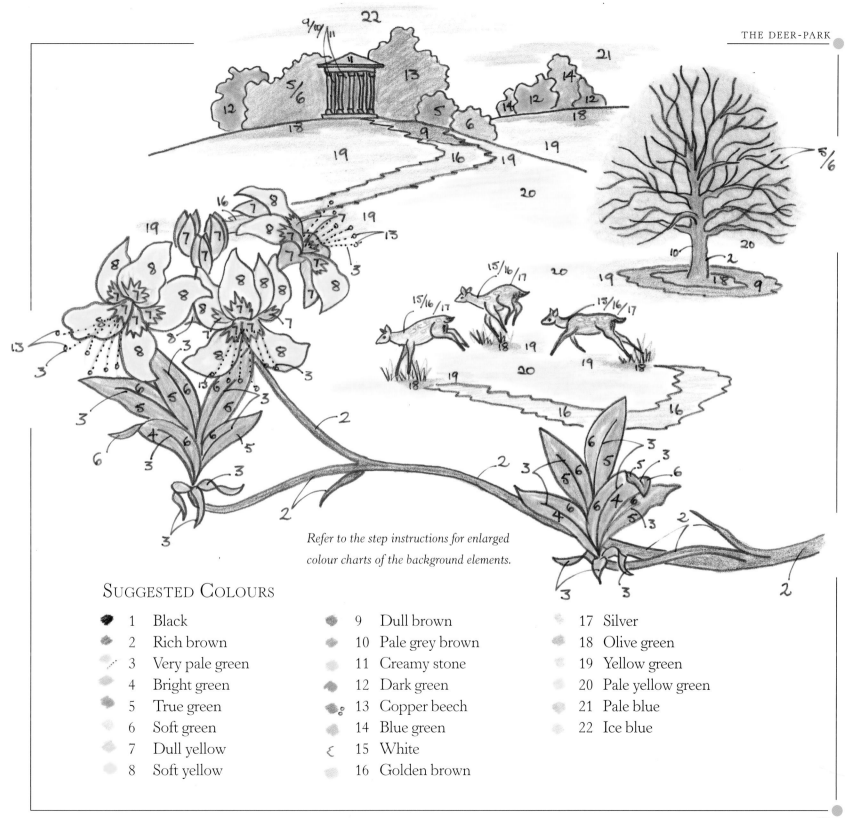

*Refer to the step instructions for enlarged
colour charts of the background elements.*

SUGGESTED COLOURS

1 Black	9 Dull brown	17 Silver
2 Rich brown	10 Pale grey brown	18 Olive green
3 Very pale green	11 Creamy stone	19 Yellow green
4 Bright green	12 Dark green	20 Pale yellow green
5 True green	13 Copper beech	21 Pale blue
6 Soft green	14 Blue green	22 Ice blue
7 Dull yellow	15 White	
8 Soft yellow	16 Golden brown	

DESIGN NOTES

The imagined light source is centrally located for the foreground element, and slightly to the left for the landscape. The deer are in movement, so their shadow lines need particularly careful attention.

BEGIN WITH THE AZALEA. . .

1 In fine stem stitch, in black (1) work the shadow line on all elements of the branch, leaves and flowers. Work the branch in snake stitch in rich brown (2). In fine stem stitch in very pale green (3) complete all the central leaf veins and the leaves themselves in directional *opus plumarium* in bright green (4), true green (5) and soft green (6). Work the basal leaflets in delicate fields of snake stitch or radial *opus plumarium*, as appropriate, in very pale green.

2 Turning to the flowers, work the inner strata of each petal in radial *opus plumarium* in dull yellow (7). Feed the outer strata into the first in soft yellow (8). Add the small areas of the flower trumpets in radial work, falling to the invisible core at the base of the rosette in dull yellow and work the buds in very lightly converging lozenges and part lozenges of radial *opus plumarium* in the same shade. (The stamens will be worked at the end of the project.)

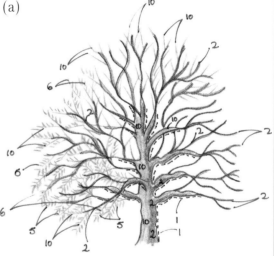

(a)

MOVING ON TO THE LANDSCAPE. . .

3 Refer to chart detail (a) as necessary. In very fine stem stitch in black, shadow line the oak tree on the underside (or side away from the light source) as suggested by the dashed line on colour chart detail (a), i.e., only on the double-sided elements of the design. Working in fine stem stitch, in rich brown and pale grey brown (10), as indicated, begin to work the outer branches, broadening the stitches into snake stitch as they approach the trunk. Sweep the stitches down into the trunk and continue with upright straight stitching – varying the shades as suggested.

4 Add the fine twigs in straight stitches in pale grey brown (top) and begin to clothe each twig and branch with seed stitches, first in soft green on the upper surface of each (middle), then adding true green underneath (bottom). Angle the seed stitches as shown.

5 Refer to chart detail (b). Shadow line the temple in straight stitches in black. In upright straight stitching, work the columns and other architectural details in creamy stone (11), pale grey brown and dull brown, adding two angled long straight stitches in creamy stone to suggest the roof. In varying shades of true green, soft green, dark green (12) and copper beech (13) work small, massed seed stitches for the surrounding trees. Leave irregular voids between the different foliages and around the temple. Angle the stitches randomly.

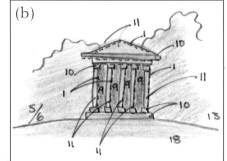

6 For the far distant trees, work upright straight stitches in dark green and blue green (14), again voiding between the various clumps.

(c)

7 Refer to chart detail (c). Shadow line the deer in fine black thread in very fine mini-stem stitch or straight stitches as appropriate, and add the eyes, also in black (right). Work mini-Dalmatian dog spots in white (15) on each deer's back and a small stratum at the base of each tail. Beginning at the head (the tip of the nose is the stitching core) work mini-radial *opus plumarium* in advancing strata, in golden brown (16), down the neck, along the back (flooding around the Dalmatian dog spots) and down the legs of each deer (middle). Complete neck, body and legs in mini-radial work in silver (17) adding small strata in black at the top of the tail and rump. Work a few mini-seed stitches in white to suggest the white rump 'flash' and angled seed stitches in dull brown for hooves. Add a minute white seed stitch to each eye (left).

(d)

Complete the landscape by working horizontal straight stitch in dull brown, golden brown, olive green (18), yellow green (19) and pale yellow green (20), adding a few angled upright stitches at the base of the oak tree and beneath the deer. Vary textures if possible, adding a suggestion of sky in pale blue (21) and ice blue (22). Finish the azalea flowers by adding long straight stitches in very pale green, tipped by seed stitches in copper beech for the stamens, overlaying landscape and other features as necessary. Finally, referring to chart detail (d), add some tiny birds in flight in fine black thread: work an 'M', thickening alternate strokes with a second, angled stitch, and adding a fine seed stitch at the centre to create each bird. Place them as you choose.

MATERIALS

FABRIC

The choice of fabric and threads can affect the ultimate appearance of any embroidery and, as with the choice of colourways, should be at the discretion of the embroiderer. However, to achieve satisfactory results, certain practical considerations need to be borne in mind.

For so-called flat-work embroidery, which must be worked in a frame, it is essential that the fabric chosen for the background does not stretch. If the fabric stretches even slightly while the embroidery is in progress, when taken out of the frame it will contract to its normal size and the embroidery will be distorted. It is also a good idea to look for a smooth, evenweave fabric. Suitable fabrics include:

* Cotton
* Polyester cotton ('Percale')
* Linen

Pure silk may also be used, but avoid types with too much 'slub' in the weave as this will interrupt the flow of the embroidery stitches.

The embroideries in this book have been worked on an inexpensive cotton/polyester fabric (sometimes called 'Percale') which is very light-weight. Poly-cotton mixes (evenweave) in a heavier weight are also ideal for use in this type of embroidery. Larger pictures should be worked on heavier fabrics, small studies on

lightweights, but this rule can be adapted to the particular needs of the work in question.

When choosing fabric, try to avoid any fabrics which have too loose a weave, as this will result in too many stitches vying for space in too few threads of warp and weft. As a general rule, if the weave is open enough to be used for counted thread embroidery, it will be too wide for us!

THREADS

A variety of threads are necessary to achieve diverse effects but the ultimate choice of which type to use on a specific area is a personal one. Any thread suitable for flat-work embroidery may be used for any of the techniques in this book. Natural fibres are easier to use than synthetics and include cotton, floss silk and twisted silk.

◀ *Pure silks and cottons are available in a glorious variety of colours and textures. Clockwise from bottom left: stranded cottons, stranded and twisted silks, Japanese floss silk, fine floss silk, spun (fine twisted) silk.*

✻ COTTON
Most embroiderers are familiar with stranded cotton. It is usually available in six-stranded skeins and strands should be used singly.

✻ FLOSS SILK
This is untwisted with a high sheen, and is also known as sleave or Japanese silk. It should be doubled or split (as appropriate to the type chosen) to match the gauge of a single strand of stranded cotton to complete most of the projects in this book.

✻ TWISTED SILK
This usually has several strands twisted together. Single strands of most twisted silks are approximately the same gauge as single strands of stranded cotton and should be used singly. Very fine details should be worked in finer gauges of thread if available.

✻ SYNTHETIC METALLIC THREADS
These are available in many formats in gold, silver and other colours. The most versatile are several stranded threads, which may be used entire where a thick gauge is required, or split into single strands for fine or delicate details.

* **'REAL' GOLD AND SILVER THREAD**
These threads are usually made using a percentage of real gold or silver. Generally they comprise very narrow strips of leaf or fine metal twisted around a synthetic, cotton or silk core. 'Passing' thread is tightly wound and available in various gauges, the finest of which may be used directly in the needle, the thicker couched down. 'Jap' gold is more loosely wound, is also available in a variety of gauges, but is usually only suitable for couching.

* **BLENDING FILAMENTS**
This term encompasses a vast number of specialist threads but usually refers to threads that are made up of a number of strands of differing types, e.g. a silky thread together with a cellophane or sparkling thread. They may be used entire, or split down into their component parts, which may then be used separately.

TOOLS

Basic embroidery tools have remained unchanged for centuries and the essentials are described here.

* **EMBROIDERY FRAME**
In flat-work embroidery the tension of the background fabric is all important (see Stitch Variations, page 92) and it is essential to work on an embroidery frame. Round, tambour hoops are best suited to fine embroidery as they produce an entirely uniform tension. Wooden hoops maintain their tension best. Always use a hoop or frame large enough to allow a generous amount of fabric around your design.

* **SCISSORS**
You will need small scissors for threads, fine and sharp. I use pinking shears for cutting fabric, which also helps to prevent fraying. Don't use thread or fabric scissors to cut anything else or you will blunt the blades.

* **NEEDLES**
These should always be chosen with the specific use of threads and fabrics in mind. 'Embroidery' needles are designed with a long eye and a sharp point. You will find a selection of sizes 5 to 10 are the most useful. Size 8 is ideal for use with a 'single strand' gauge as discussed above.

▼ *Floss and twisted silk produce different effects: glossy, as shown on the plant and upper sides of the butterflies' wings, or with the subtler, matt glow illustrated by the underside of the wings.*
10.75 x 12.75cm (4½ x 5in)

▲ *Metallic and specialist materials. Clockwise from top left: imitation gold thread (stranded), real gold passing thread, coloured metallic threads, real silver passing thread, blending filaments, imitation silver thread (stranded) with bugle and seed beads.*

▲ *Working in stranded cotton and imitation metallic thread can create a soft, muted effect.*
10 x 12.75cm (4 x 5in)

HELEN M. STEVENS

BASIC TECHNIQUES

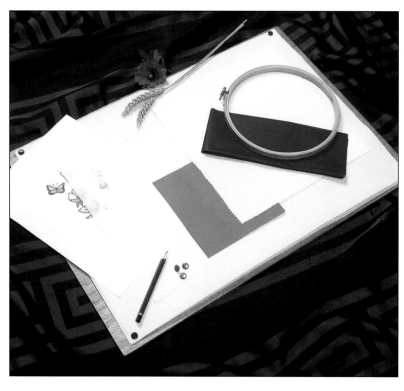

Before you begin to embroider it is important to pay attention to the initial preparation and transfer of your design. Similarly, after your project is completed you need to give some thought to the presentation of the work.

TRANSFERRING A DESIGN

You will need (see picture above, left to right):
* Original design
* Tracing paper (use good quality, about 90gsm)
* 'H' pencil
* Drawing pins
* Dressmakers' carbon paper in a colour contrasting your fabric
* Fabric
* Tissue paper
* Tambour hoop

You will also need scissors and a smooth, hard surface on which to work. Ideally, this should be a wooden drawing board covered with several layers of lining paper.

1 Place the tracing paper over your design and carefully trace off the design, omitting any very fine details, e.g., whiskers, spiders' webs, butterflies' antennae. These lines, if transferred, could not be covered by single strands of thread and must be added freehand during the course of the embroidery.

2 Lay your fabric flat, and place the tracing on top of it. Carefully pin the tracing in place with two drawing pins at the top right and left corners. Interleave between fabric and tracing paper with

the carbon (colour side down) and hold secure with a third drawing pin through the tracing at the bottom of the paper. Do not pin through the carbon.

With a firm, even pressure, use a pencil to re-draw each line of the design. After you have completed a few lines of the design, carefully lift one corner of the tracing paper and carbon paper to check that your design is being successfully transferred.

3 When the transfer is complete, remove the bottom drawing pin, lift back the tracing and remove the carbon paper. Check that every detail of the design has been transferred before finally removing the tracing paper. You are now ready to mount your fabric, using tissue paper and a tambour hoop (see instructions opposite).

MOUNTING FABRIC IN A TAMBOUR HOOP

You will need:
* Fabric, with the design transferred
* Tissue paper
* Tambour hoop

1 Cut two sheets of tissue paper at least 5cm (2in) wider than the outer dimensions of your tambour hoop. Place the inner ring of your hoop on a flat surface and lay one sheet of tissue paper over it. Lay your fabric over the tissue paper, and ensure that the design is centred in the ring. Lay a second sheet of tissue paper over the fabric and slip the outer ring of the hoop over the entire 'sandwich'. Tighten the screw until the fabric and paper is held firmly.

2 Trim the upper sheet of tissue paper inside and outside the upper ring (as shown above). Now turn the hoop over and trim the lower sheet of tissue paper similarly. The tissue paper will protect your fabric from abrasion by the hoop and keep the handled edges clean. You are now ready to begin your embroidery.

MOUNTING AND FRAMING YOUR WORK

You will need (see picture above):
* Backing board (rigid cardboard, foamboard or hardboard)
* Acid free cartridge paper (cut to the same size as the backing board)
* Lacing thread (a mercerised cotton is recommended)
* Two crewel needles (large enough to take your chosen cotton)
* Scissors

1 When your embroidery is complete press it on the wrong side, without steam (after checking the manufacturer's instructions for fabric and thread). Always press through another piece of fabric, and be *particularly* careful if you have used blending or other specialist filaments, especially cellophane threads.

It is essential to mount your work under similar tension to that exerted on the fabric whilst in the hoop. Lace it firmly on to a rigid backing board to achieve this tension. Make sure your backing board is large enough to take the whole design, with enough space at each edge to allow for framing.

2 Place the cartridge paper carefully between the board and the fabric. Next, position your embroidery, always making sure that the warp/weft of the fabric lies straight in relation the edges of the board.

3 Invert the ensemble so that the embroidery is face down, with the cartridge paper and board on top of it. Cut the fabric to size, with a comfortable overlap. Fold the two sides in toward the board centre. Cut a long but manageable piece of lacing thread and thread a needle at each end, leaving two 'tails' of similar length.

Working from the top, insert a needle on either side and lace the two sides of the fabric together, in corset fashion, until you reach the bottom. If you run out of thread simply tie the thread off and begin again.

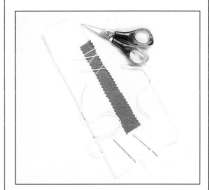

4 Fold the top and bottom of the fabric toward the centre and repeat the lacing process. Always tie off the ends of the lacing thread with firm, non-slip knots and snip off any extra thread that is left. It takes a little practise to achieve the perfect tension.

Do not over tighten the laces as the thread may break, or rip the fabric, but do not be afraid to exert a reasonable pull on the work as only in this way will the original tension of the fabric on the tambour hoop be re-created.

5 The choice of framing is a personal matter, but always be prepared to take professional advice as the framing can make or mar a picture. A window mount is a good idea to keep the glass away from the fabric (and is essential if beads or thick specialist threads have been used) and remember that a frame should complement rather than dominate your design.

STITCH VARIATIONS

The stitches in this book are a combination of traditional embroidery stitches and contemporary innovations. They are flexible and adaptable: a single basic stitch such as stem stitch, depending on how it is applied, can produce a variety of effects, from a fine, sinuous line to a broad, strong one, with an infinite choice of widths, curves and reflexes within each variation.

The stitches fall into several distinct categories – linear, filling and decorative. Each has its own special properties and is suited to the description of certain shapes, fields and textures.

When working on a hoop the fabric must be taut within the frame. Stitches are always worked by the 'stab and pull' method. The needle is pushed through the fabric from above, the embroiderer's hand then moves to the back and pulls the needle through the fabric so the stitch forms smoothly on the surface. The next stitch is begun by pushing the needle up through the fabric from the reverse of the work, the hand is brought to the front to pull the needle through, prior to beginning the routine once again.

LINEAR STITCHES

1 STEM STITCH
Always work from the top of any line to be described (on a natural history subject the outer extremity). Work *with* the curve of the subject: bring your needle out just to the outside of the curve and put it in on the inside of the curve.

a Fine/narrow stem stitch
Overlap the stitches by only a small proportion of the stitch length. The line created is only the width of a single stitch, creating a fine, sinuous effect.

b Broad stem stitch
Overlap the stitches so that half to three-quarters of each stitch lies beside its neighbour. The juxtaposition of several stitches creates a thick, strong effect.

c Graduating stem stitch
Begin with a fine stem stitch, increase it to a one-half ratio, then to three-quarters ratio within the same line creating a gradually thickening line (like a growing stem – narrower at the tip, broader at the base).

d Coiling stem stitch
Begin with small stitches to describe the tight curve at the centre of the coil and gradually lengthen the stitches as the curve becomes gentler.

e Reflexing stem stitch
Beginning at the tip of the line, work the chosen variation a–c until the direction of the curve begins to change. Take one straight stitch through the preceding stitch, along the pattern line. Begin the stem stitch again, bringing the needle up on the new outside of the curve.

2 STRAIGHT STITCH
There are occasions when a completely straight line in the pattern can be described by a simple, straight stitch, or when a large field of the design must be filled smoothly with abutting straight stitches, such as in landscape work. The fabric must be taut within your frame to work this technique successfully.

a Vertical straight stitch (long)
Work this stitch from the top down. Usually the stitches will be angled toward their base, such as in the case of simple grass effects. Ensure the stitch completely covers the transfer line.

b Horizontal straight stitch (long)
This stitch is used in blocks to suggest landscape effects. Work toward any abutting groups of stitches. To suggest a break in perspective, void (see 4, right) between abutting fields. To blend shades within a single field, stitch into the abutting field.

c Free straight stitch (long or short)
Fine details, such as whiskers, do not appear as transferred pattern lines (see Basic Techniques, page 90). These can be worked freehand in straight stitches angled to suit the particular needs of the subject matter. Work away from abutting groups of stitches.

3 SHADOW LINING
Establish the direction of the imagined light source within your picture. Each element of the design away from this light source will be shadow lined. Put a pin in the work, its tip pointing in the direction of the light source, to remind you of its origin.

a Smooth shadow lining
Work a fine, accurate stem stitch along the pattern line, just to its underside.

b Fragmented shadow lining
Where a line is too irregular to permit shadow lining by stem stitch, use straight stitches tailored to the length of the section of outline to be described.

4 VOIDING
Where two fields of a filling technique abut (see below), with or without a shadow line, suggesting that one element of the design overlaps another, a narrow line void of stitching should be left between the two. In practice, this forms on the transferred pattern line dividing the two elements. It should be approximately as wide as the gauge of thread used for the embroidery itself. To check that the width is correct, loosely position a strand of the thread along the 'valley' of the void. If it fits snugly, the width is correct.

FILLING STITCHES

1 OPUS PLUMARIUM
This literally means 'feather work' and emulates the way in which feathers lie smoothly, yet with infinite changes of direction, upon a bird's body. The angle of the stitches sweeps around without breaking the flow of the stitching itself and this in turn catches the light, refracting it back from the stitching and giving a three-dimensional impression.

a Radial opus plumarium
(single or first stratum)
Begin with a stitch central to the field to be covered. This, and all subsequent stitches, are worked from the *outer* edge of the transferred pattern line *inwards* toward the centre of the motif. Bring the needle out immediately adjacent to the top of the first stitch. Slip the needle beneath the first stitch and through the fabric about two-thirds of the way down its length. This advances the angle of the stitching.

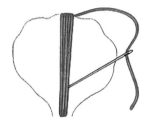

Subsequent stitches can be either full length or shorter and angled as described, allowing the embroidery to fan out and cover the field without too many stitches bunching up at the inner core of the motif. A gradual advancement of the angle is achieved by working the angled stitches longer (e.g., three-quarters of the length of full stitches); more acute advancement of the angle by working them shorter (one quarter to one half of the length of the full stitches).

b Radial opus plumarium
(subsequent strata)
Where a broad field of stitches is required to fill a motif, several strata of *opus plumarium* may be required.

Work the first stratum by the single stratum method described above. Always stitching *inwards* (toward the core of the motif), work the second stratum by taking a first stitch at the centre of the field. Stitch into the first stratum (do not leave a void) and, following the established flow of the stitching, fan out on either side of the first stitch, advancing the angle when necessary, as before. Subsequent strata are worked similarly.

c Directional opus plumarium
(single or first stratum)
Where the core of the motif is elongated (such as the central vein of a simple elliptic leaf) the stitches should flow smoothly along its length. Again, always stitch inwards, bringing the needle out at the outer edge of the motif and in toward its centre.

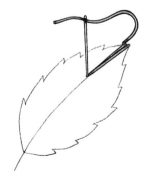

Begin at the tip of the motif (or outer extremity of the first stratum) and take the first stitch inwards to abut the tip of the elongated core. Work your way down the field to be covered advancing the angle as necessary, as described above (a).

d Directional opus plumarium
(subsequent strata)
Work the first strata as described above. Again working from the direction of the tip of the motif inwards, create subsequent strata by stitching into the previous stratum (do not void), advancing the angle of the stitching as necessary to match the abutting stitches.

2 OPPOSITE ANGLE STITCHING
This is used to create the effect of reflex, e.g., where a leaf or petal curls forward or backward to reveal its underside.

Following the principles of *opus plumarium* work the stitches at an exactly opposite angle to the abutting field. (Occasionally the angles will be similar in actuality, but opposite in relation to the concept of the directional stitching.) Where necessary void between the two.

3 SNAKE STITCH
This is used to describe long, sinuous shapes, such as broad blades of grass or other linear leaves.

a Simple snake stitch
Begin at the tip of the motif, taking the first stitch in the direction of the curve to be described. For subsequent stitches, bring the needle out on the *outside* of the curve and in on the *inside*.

Work smoothly down the motif, advancing the angle of stitches, if necessary, by the *opus plumarium* method and lengthening the stitches where appropriate, as with graduating stem stitch (see above).

b Reflexing snake stitch
Begin at the point of reflex, where the direction of the curve changes. First, take a stitch angled across the field slanting between the tip and base of the curve.

Work upwards to the tip, bringing the needle out on the outside of the curve and in on the inside until the upper field is complete. Advance the angle of stitching by the *opus plumarium* method if necessary. Complete the lower field by returning to the central stitch and working down the motif, again bringing the needle out on the outside and in on the inside of the curve. Advance the stitch angle as necessary.

4 DALMATION DOG TECHNIQUE

This is used to create a single, smooth field of embroidery where an area of one colour is completely encompassed by another colour. Used within *opus plumarium* (either radial or directional).

a Simple Dalmatian dog

Establish the radial or directional flow of the *opus plumarium*. Working the stitches at exactly the same angle as the main field of *opus plumarium* to follow, work the spots or other fields to be covered first. When completed, flood the rest of the *opus plumarium* around them, again paying careful attention to the flow of the stitches.

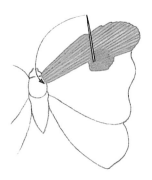

b Multiple Dalmatian dog

This technique can create a 'spot within a spot' or any other irregular pattern.

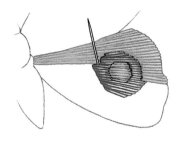

Establish either the radial or directional flow of the *opus plumarium*. Maintaining the angle of stitching as above, work the innermost colour first, followed by outer field or fields of colour until the spots or other shapes are complete. Flood the surrounding *opus plumarium* around them.

DECORATIVE STITCHING

1 SEED STITCH

Fine, short, straight stitches worked directly on to the fabric, occasionally superimposed over other embroidery.

2 TICKING

These are seed stitches overlaying *opus plumarium*, worked at exactly the same angle as the underlying work but taken in the opposite direction, i.e., against the flow of the work.

3 STUDDING

These are seed stitches which overlay *opus plumarium*, but are worked at right angles to the underlying stitches.

4 SHOOTING STITCH

Long straight stitches taken in the opposite direction to the underlying radial or directional work.

5 CHEVRON STITCH

Two long straight stitches are angled to meet. Infill with a third straight stitch if necessary. To create a very sharp angle (such as a thistle spike) work a fourth straight stitch in a fine gauge of thread through the body of the motif.

6 DOTTING/SPECKLING

Work very short straight stitches, only as long as the width of the thread, to create an impression of tiny round dots. Work the stitches close together and in random directions.

7 FLOATING EMBROIDERY

This allows the threads to lie loosely on the fabric, falling into spontaneous shapes. Do not transfer the design to be formed on to the background fabric.

Take a long stitch from the inside to the outside of the motif, putting a finger or pencil under the thread to keep it away from the fabric. Take a very small stitch at the outer point of the motif to bring the thread back to the

surface. Take a third stitch back to the core of the motif, again keeping a finger beneath the thread. Repeat the process, removing the finger or pencil when several strands have built up.

8 SURFACE COUCHING

Usually a goldwork technique, this can be used effectively on various threads.

Bring the thread to be couched (the base thread) through the fabric to the surface of the work. If it is too thick to be brought through the fabric, lay it in place and hold it down with a thumb. Thread a second needle with a finer thread (the couching thread) and bring it up through the fabric immediately alongside the base thread. Take a tiny stitch over the base thread, at right angles to it, and repeat at regular intervals, effectively using the couching thread to whip the base thread into place along the transferred pattern line. Pay particular attention to whipping the beginning and the end of the base thread into place if it is lying wholly on the surface of the work.

9 SUBDUED VOIDING

Where two fields of *opus plumarium* abut and are separated by a voided line, the effect can be softened by working fine straight stitches, at the angle of the underlying work, across the void. Use a shade similar to that of the embroidered field 'closer' in perspective to the viewer, e.g., where a bird's wing lies over its body, or the angle of its neck creates a break in perspective. Work the overlying stitches at regular intervals, allowing the voided line to show through.

SUPPLIERS

There are many manufacturers and suppliers of embroidery materials and equipment and I have suggested a few here.
* This indicates suppliers who will accept orders direct from the given address via mail order.

Coats Crafts UK
PO Box 22, The Lingfield Estate,
McMullen Road, Darlington,
Co. Durham DL1 1YQ, UK
tel: 01325 365457
Stranded cottons

Coats and Clark
Consumer Services
PO Box 12229
Greenville, SC 29612-0229, USA
tel: (800) 648 1479
www.coatsandclark.com
Stranded cottons and fabrics

DMC Creative World Ltd.
Pullman Road, Wigston,
Leicestershire LE18 2DY, UK
tel: 0116 281 1040
fax: 0116 281 3592
www.dmc/cw.com
*Stranded cotton, imitation
gold and silver threads*

DMC Corporation
Building 10, Port Kearny,
South Kearny, NJ 07032, USA
tel: (US) 201 589 0606
*Stranded cotton, imitation gold
and silver threads*

Japanese Embroidery Centre UK *
White Lodge, Littlewick Road,
Lower Knaphill, Woking,
Surrey GU21 2JU, UK
tel: 01483 476246
*Floss silk, real gold and silver threads,
imitation gold, silver and coloured
metallic threads*

Kreinik Manufacturing. Co., Inc.
3106 Timanus Lane, Suite 101,
Baltimore, MD 21244, USA
tel: (US) 800 537 2166
(UK ++01325 365 457)
www.kreinik.com
email: kreinik@kreinik.com
*Silks, blending filaments and
metallic threads*

Madeira Threads (UK) Ltd.
PO Box 6, Thirsk,
North Yorkshire YO7 3BX, UK
tel: 01845 524880
www.madeira.co.uk
email: acts@madeira
Twisted/stranded silks

Pearsall's
Tancrad Street, Taunton,
Somerset TA1 1RY, UK
tel: 01823 274700
Shop online at
www.pearsallsembroidery.com
Stranded pure silk threads

Pipers Specialist Silks *
Chinnerys, Egremont Street,
Glemsford, Sudbury,
Suffolk CI10 7SA, UK
tel: 01787 280920
www.pipers-silks.com
email: susanpeck@pipers-silks.com
*Floss and spun (twisted) silk. Exclusive silk
kits designed by Helen M. Stevens*

Stephen Simpson Ltd. *
50 Manchester Road,
Preston PR1 3YH, UK
tel: 01772 556688
Real gold and silver threads

The Voirrey Embroidery Centre *
Brimstage Hall,
Wirral L63 6JA, UK
tel: 0151 3423514
General embroidery supplies

Helen M. Stevens
Lectures, masterclasses and themed
holidays are available based around
Helen's work. For full details of these
and other products and activities,
including masterclass lessons online,
visit: www.helenmstevens.co.uk

Alternatively, contact Helen via
David & Charles, Brunel House,
Forde Close, Newton Abbot, Devon,
TQ12 4PU, UK

ACKNOWLEDGMENTS

Thank you to all those who have been a part of this book, friends too numerous to mention who have added their comments to the gardening theme! On the practical side, thanks to Cheryl and the team at David & Charles, especially to Lin Clements and to Pam, Nigel and Angela for all their usual support. For the whiskers and inspiration in Plate 21, thanks, Taffy! Plate 4 first appeared in *Classic Inspirations* magazine, published by Country Bumpkin, and Plate 5 is by kind permission of 'Paro'.

INDEX

Italic page numbers indicate plates; **bold** page numbers indicate figures.

STITCHES AND TECHNIQUES